D1162637

THIS IS
BAKER'S CLAY

THIS IS BAKER'S CLAY
A New Sculpture/Craft Medium

Molli Nickell

Illustrations by Marlo Johansen
Photography by Molli Nickell

DRAKE PUBLISHERS INC.   NEW YORK

Library of Congress Cataloging in Publication Data

Nickell, Molli.
   This is baker's clay.

   1. Modeling.   I. Title.
NB1180.N54   731.4'2   73-5550
ISBN 0-87749-525-4

Printed in Brazil

Printed and Bound by
Gráfica Editora Primor S.A.
Rio de Janeiro - GB - Brazil

Paper: Suzano-Feffer Group

In memory of my father
Charles H. McIntyre, M.D.

CONTENTS

THIS IS
BAKER'S CLAY

1 ON BEING CREATIVE

Now that you've thumbed your way through the book and eyeballed the projects, you may be thinking that Baker's Clay does indeed look like fun, but you say, "I'm not all that creative. How can I hope to make lovelies like these?" Never let a negative notion prevent you from having hours (or years) of fun creating Baker's Clay inedibles. Nearly all of us are creative creatures whether we are aware of it or not. Unfortunately, through some unhappy process of indoctrination, we have been conditioned to think that if we don't have a college degree in art, then we simply cannot consider ourselves creative or work in a craft media more advanced than Paper Dolls II.

Have you ever baked a cake? Staged a birthday party? Curled your hair? Put up the hem on a new dress? Wrapped a gift? Probably you've tackled several of these activities, activities which have one thing in common: they bring something into being, which is the dictionary definition for "creativity." So pat yourself on the back for possessing talent you never gave yourself credit for having and take a good look at your creative assets—two hands, a mind, an oven, a kitchen full of assorted craftiments like flour, salt, glue, scissors, cookie sheet—and this book. Take it from me: you *can* make absolutely anything you see here (and lots of things you'll dream up by yourself) from Baker's Clay.

If you still have doubts, take a look at some case histories of a gang of goof-offs who banded interests and abilities together to bring you this book. All of these gals have worked successfully with Baker's Clay and other craft media, and none has had formal training in art.

1

Jahn Ruhl, city planner, wife of Irv the psychologist, and mother to two little girls and two mop dogs.

Marlo Johansen, whose college major was chemistry with
an M.A. in bugs (that's entomology, and although she is
a whiz at telling the sex of a mosquito at ten paces, she
usually doesn't talk about it), is married to Don the Phar-
macist, mother to three smallish female children and a cat.

Sandie Piper, instructor of library skills, married to
author/teacher Jim, mother to two small boys, two dogs,
a horse and a new-born filly.

Jerrie Peters, registered nurse, wife of Bob the doctor and mother of three assorted children, three dogs, five birds, increasing numbers of white mice and several transient cats.

All led, or prodded by me, a college dropout whose interests prior to crafts were changing diapers and daily survival.

Common denominators for our little group are husbands, children, pets, station wagons, proper suburban homes, mountains of unironed clothes, and the common need to find personal identity. Most young mothers go through this at one time or another; some take up golf or skydiving; others learn to play bridge or cultivate petunias; some start drinking or flirting with the mailman; and others find the needed identity by becoming involved in the creative world of handicrafts. Good-deed activities like scouts and PTA bazaars brought us together, and we discovered our common love for things hand-made. We shared our creative interest during weekly crafting sessions as we learned to make all sorts of interesting things to offer for sale at various fund-raising functions. We were constantly invited to demonstrate Baker's Clay and other craft processes to ladies' clubs and assorted organizations and finally came to the conclusion that others like ourselves might enjoy becoming involved with creative handwork. Others like you, maybe? Perhaps we had better warn you before you begin, because once you start on the path of creative enjoyment, your household may not be as well organized, floors may not shine as brightly, and shirts certainly will not be ironed as often. On the other hand, like thousands of others who have discovered Baker's Clay, you will uncover a new you, a new enjoyment of doing something with and for family and friends, just as you will feel the excitement and fulfillment of actually making something frivolous, something fun or something useful with your own hands.

The little ol' dough maker

ABOUT BAKER'S CLAY 2

Congratulations! You are about to become a sculptor,—perhaps not Michelangelo, but enough of a craft person to make dozens of charming, three-dimensional decorator goodies. But unlike other sculptors, you won't be working in the conventional forms of stone, plaster or clay. Instead, you'll work with—of all things—a salt and flour mixture, a special kind of clay dough called Baker's Clay which is easy to work with and reasonably permanent. This book will be your guide to a whole new world of handicrafted pieces made with Baker's Clay.

This delightful medium was probably invented by a frustrated Renaissance housewife whose kids couldn't go out to play because of the plague. Much like the homemaker of today, she had to find something therapeutic and absorbing to amuse active little minds and inquisitive fingers. When she discovered Baker's Clay, she found something to absorb herself, too. Some techniques from those early days of Baker's Clay remain with us, but several twentieth-century innovations are now used to make the finished pieces durable and strong enough to last the next 400 years. If your inquiring mind demands more historical insight into the origin of Baker's Clay, look it up under "breads" in your local encyclopedia.

You can baste Baker's Clay with milk to make it look like leather; paint it to resemble pottery; spray it with metallic paints to look like metal sculpture; or leave it natural to look like Baker's Clay. No other craft medium is so versatile or requires less knowledge and so few tools. To master the few basic techniques of Baker's Clay, all you need are a kitchen, a few baking tools like a rolling pin, cookie sheet and oven, and a strong and enthusiastic desire to create something with your own hands.

Perhaps the best thing about Baker's Clay is its low cost and the ready availability of the few necessary supplies. (Also, it provides a good way to use up flour that is inhabited by weevils). Flour and salt are quite inexpensive, and if you use paint sparingly, you can work for months and months in this media with a too-small-to-mention outlay for materials—a claim that can't be made by any craft form around. And even though the projects don't cost anything at all to make, they end up looking like they did! You probably have enough of the basics in your kitchen right now. After your home is filled with Baker's Clay projects, you will find that the pieces are charming enough to use as small gifts, to sell in specialty shops, or to donate to bazaars or other good-deed fund-raising functions.

As you thumb your way through this book to check out the projects and ideas, you'll notice that many of the finished pieces have been given names or titles. You may think that this practice is a bit silly, and maybe it is. However, after you've started making things from Baker's Clay, you'll find that certain projects end up becoming family favorites, and like the kids, cat or goldfish, need to be named.

Beauty on couch waiting for the Beast.

And So Before You Begin

There are certain necessary tidbits of information which you'll want to pick up as you work with Baker's Clay. Projects are included so you can make and bake something while you learn to master each technique.

9

Some of these basic techniques include preparing the dough, deciding what to do with it, baking it and painting it. Also included are brainstorming ideas and suggestions on how you can switch around methods and techniques to make an endless assortment of unique Baker's Clay pieces.

It helps to be a bit of a philosopher when working with the dough. You must be willing to let the dough "do its own thing" once you pop it into the oven, because at this point you lose some control. Baker's Clay, while in the oven, will occasionally brown, bubble and curl unpredictably, adding an element of surprise to your endeavors. Accept the fact that you are not in total control and you will quickly learn to enjoy the warmth and charm of the results even though your *pièce d'resistance* looks a little different than you had envisioned. Scattered discreetly throughout the book are descriptions of disasters of one sort or another, some caused by initial lack of knowledge and experience in working with Baker's Clay. Perhaps you should consider adopting a type of crafting philosophy that won't allow setbacks and dum-dum mistakes distract you from learning how to do something enjoyable, but instead will help you learn something from every disaster, whether it be a moldy angel or a shattered wall plaque. So when something goes awry with a project you've been working on, don't despair, repair if possible, and bake on. Somewhere in this book you'll probably find reference to a similar disaster, then you can exercise your option either to remedy the problem, accept and love it "as is," or toss the whole thing in the trash can.

Should you be one of those whose lifetime motto is "after all else fails, read the directions," then forge ahead, and come back later after your first disaster.

So relax, pour yourself a cup of coffee or glass of your favorite spirits and prepare to enter the magic land of white thumb and floury floor.

3 HOW TO MAKE BAKER'S CLAY

Preparing the Dough

This is the tried-and-true recipe for Baker's Clay dough. Before you mix up your first batch, please read *all* the basic information in this chapter, then after you get the gist of how to mix it up and what to do with it after that, make something following the easy step-by-step directions in the next chapter.

Recipe For Baker's Clay

1 cup salt
1½ cups hot water
4 cups all-purpose flour

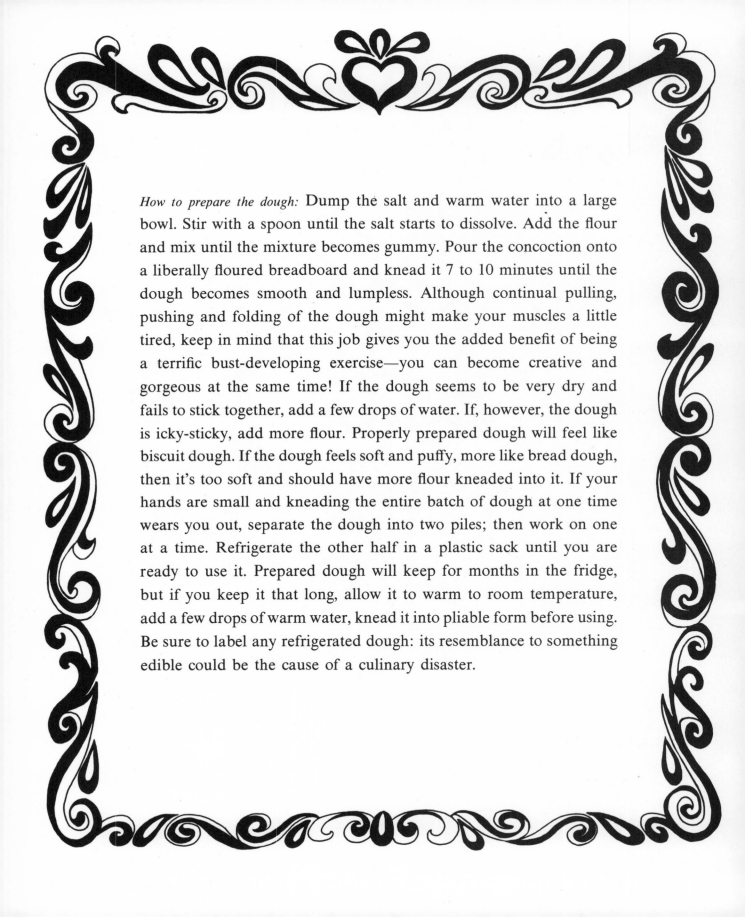

How to prepare the dough: Dump the salt and warm water into a large bowl. Stir with a spoon until the salt starts to dissolve. Add the flour and mix until the mixture becomes gummy. Pour the concoction onto a liberally floured breadboard and knead it 7 to 10 minutes until the dough becomes smooth and lumpless. Although continual pulling, pushing and folding of the dough might make your muscles a little tired, keep in mind that this job gives you the added benefit of being a terrific bust-developing exercise—you can become creative and gorgeous at the same time! If the dough seems to be very dry and fails to stick together, add a few drops of water. If, however, the dough is icky-sticky, add more flour. Properly prepared dough will feel like biscuit dough. If the dough feels soft and puffy, more like bread dough, then it's too soft and should have more flour kneaded into it. If your hands are small and kneading the entire batch of dough at one time wears you out, separate the dough into two piles; then work on one at a time. Refrigerate the other half in a plastic sack until you are ready to use it. Prepared dough will keep for months in the fridge, but if you keep it that long, allow it to warm to room temperature, add a few drops of warm water, knead it into pliable form before using. Be sure to label any refrigerated dough: its resemblance to something edible could be the cause of a culinary disaster.

(FIGURE 12) Dump all ingredients into a bowl and mix until everything becomes gummy.

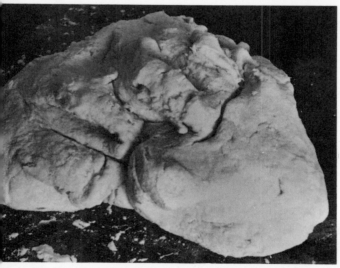

(FIGURE 13) Pour the concoction onto a liberally floured breadboard and start kneading it. This is how it will look after two minutes.

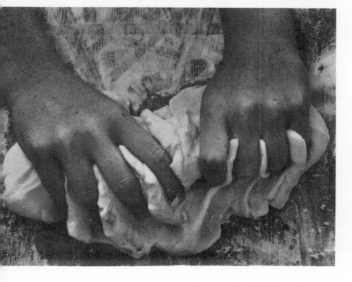

(FIGURE 14) The dough has been kneaded for ten minutes. It needs to have a little more flour worked into it, because it is *too soft*.

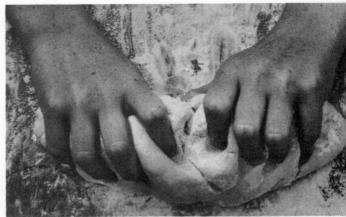

(FIGURE 15) This dough has been kneaded for ten minutes. It needs to have a few drops of water kneaded into it because it is *too hard*.

(FIGURE 16) This dough has been kneaded for ten minutes. It looks and feels like biscuit dough and is *just right* (said Goldilocks).

The Lump and You, or What To Do with Prepared Baker's Clay Dough

(FIGURE 17) There the lump sits, just daring you to be creative. It shouldn't take you long to familiarize yourself with working with the dough. Some of the most basic and simple techniques involve flattening, imprinting, and layering.

Look over these simple steps. Once you have mixed up a batch of dough and kneaded it to the proper consistency you can:

Flatten It

Work on a floured breadboard as you roll the dough out to ½-inch thickness, using a rolling-pin or empty

Figure 17

14

glass bottle. After you decide what you are going to make, draw the outline on the dough using a toothpick or some other equally sophisticated sculpture tool. You may feel that ½-inch dough is too thick or unwieldy, while actually this is the absolute minimum thickness with which you should work to get good results at first. Dough that is thinner than ½-inch is tricky to handle, as I shall explain later on.

Cut It

Cut the drawn shape out with your kitchen knife, then lift the piece with a spatula and place it on your teflon or foil-covered cookie sheet. If you don't have a nonstick cookie sheet, treat yourself to one, so that you won't have to fuss with covering it with aluminum foil every time you want to work on Baker's Clay.

Draw on It

Imprint or scratch designs on the cut-out shape using a variety of implements like toothpicks, bottle caps, hair pins, table utensils, and other modeling and decorating tools which you'll find in and around the house (see Fig. 18). After you have finished decorating the surface of the object, push a hairpin into the top to make a dandy hanger-upper for later on.

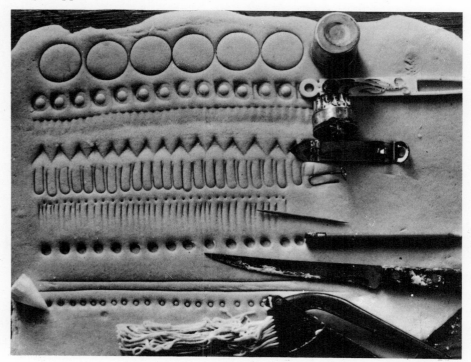

Figure 18

If you are using the oven for something practical, like baking a cake or making dinner, put plastic wrap over the Baker's Clay pieces, leave them on the cookie sheet and place in the refrigerator. This keeps the dough from drying out until it is baked. The dough you cut the shape from will become dry on top if left uncovered for 20 to 25 minutes—even quicker on a hot summer day. Keep the dough surface smooth and moist by placing aluminum foil or plastic wrap over the portion you're working with at the moment. Or fill a perfume atomizer or spray bottle with water and mist lightly over the dough every 15 minutes to keep it moist and workable. If you get all wrapped up in what you're doing and forget about the unused portion of dough (like I usually do), the surface will become flaky, crusty and dry, and you won't be able to cut pieces out of it very easily. You'll be better off wadding the dough up in a ball, adding a few drops of water, kneading for a couple of minutes, flattening it out and beginning again.

Layer It

It's easy to shape separate pieces of dough, then stick them all together to form three-dimensional pieces. First moisten the touching surfaces, then press the pieces together. You have the option of licking the dough or dabbing it with a wet paintbrush. Unless you really like salt, keep a paintbrush handy in a bowl of water. Occasionally layered pieces will separate during baking. Stick them back together (when cool) using dabs of white glue.

Bake It

Preheat your oven to 300° and bake ½-inch thick pieces for 1½ to 2 hours. Check for doneness by tapping the dough with your fingernail or a fork. The dough will give off a definite *tong* if cooked throughout, a *plumbt* if not. Unless instructions indicate differently, bake all projects described in the book at 300°. Different oven temperatures affect the dough and the final appearance of the piece in different ways. Temperature variables will be discussed in detail when future projects call for different baking times and different temperatures. All you need to know for the moment is that Baker's Clay has a tendency to bubble while baking. If you are working with pieces ½-inch or thicker and bake them at 300°, there will be only minimal bubbling. However, if the same pieces are baked at 350°, they will surely develop lots of lumps and bumps. There are cures for these lumps which occur during the baking process, and if they really bother you, pat them with a potholder or prick them with a pin (allowing the trapped moisture inside to escape). If these techniques don't work on the lumps, jump up and down and scream a bit, then place a garden rock on the lumps to hold them down while the dough bakes. If, after all your efforts, the lumps remain, try to keep calm and accept your fate. Bumps can be charming and an illustration of this point is the lovely expression which puffed up while "Ol Sol" on page 44 was baking. Careful planning couldn't have created such a concerned expression.

(FIGURE 19) Lumps, bumps and that "warpy" look in this owl and the cow seen in Plate 15 give the pieces much more charm than if they had baked perfectly flat and flawless. In short, the lesson to be learned here is to love your lumps.

Underbaked Baker's Clay will crumble, grow moldy and otherwise turn out unsatisfactorily, so it is to your advantage to make sure each piece is thoroughly baked before you remove it from the oven. Should you be working on Baker's Clay during a humid summer afternoon, try baking at 200° (so as not to heat up the kitchen), but bake the pieces two or three hours longer to compensate for the lowered temperature. If you have any doubt about whether a flattened project is really cooked in the middle, wait until the piece cools somewhat, then grasp it firmly in the center and squeeze. If the piece gives at all, or seems soft in the center, pop it back in the oven for another hour or so to cook the center section.

Figure 19

Color It

Baker's Clay turns a variety of different colors while baking, depending upon the time the pieces are in the oven, the oven temperature, the relative humidity, etc. Basting the dough with canned evaporated milk during the last 30 minutes of baking will produce a light brown leathery look. As the milk cools it turns brown and gives the Baker's Clay surface a slightly glossy sheen. Basting longer than 30 minutes creates a deeper, richer brown color. Try experimenting with basting to achieve different looks with different pieces. For example, baste a piece 20 minutes after you pop it in the oven and every 30 minutes thereafter. The finish will be super-dark, rich brown like the sun face in Plate 5. If you have spent a lot of time imprinting or putting detail into a

17

piece which you decide to baste more than once, the detail will disappear due to the darkness, but it can easily be restored using a simple painting trick which I'll explain later. You can paint Baker's Clay to make it resemble almost any material. This information is covered later in Chapter 10. For the moment, however, enjoy the honey-brown color and warm, natural appearance of your first Baker's Clay projects.

Seal It

Remove yourself and your cooled creation outdoors and spray the entire piece thoroughly with clear resin or polyurethane varnish. Be sure to flip it over and spray the back side as well. Baker's Clay tends to absorb moisture from the air, and if left unsealed will disintegrate or grow its own crop of penicillin (mold). Some projects look best sprayed with several coats of varnish to make them shiny, while others look best covered with only one coat of a matte or low-gloss varnish. You can make this choice for yourself, although some projects need products which will be mentioned.

4 FLATTENING I- SIMPLE PROJECTS

Just to make sure that you fully understand the simple steps, mix up a batch of dough and make yourself something simple, like a mushroom cluster. Whether you actually need a mushroom cluster or not isn't important, you can always give it away to a friend—the important thing is to actually put to practice the information I've covered so far.

Step One: Preheat the oven to 300°.

(FIGURE 21) *Step Two:* Roll the prepared dough to ½-inch thickness on a floured breadboard. Use a toothpick or knife tip and lightly draw the mushroom cluster outline on the dough.

(FIGURE 22) *Step Three:* Use a sharp knife to cut the shape out, then place it on your cookie sheet. If your cookie sheet is not teflon-coated, cover it with a piece of aluminum foil.

Figure 21

Figure 22

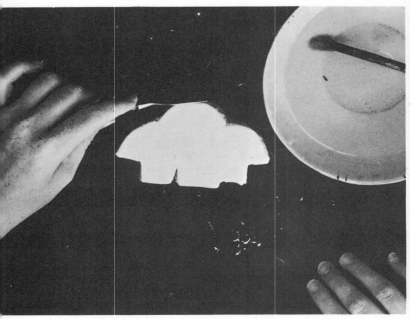

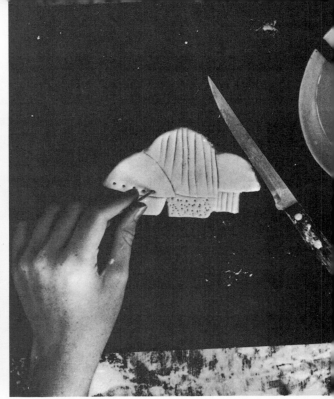

(FIGURE 23) *Step Four:* Dampen your finger or a knife blade and smooth all cut edges.

(FIGURE 24) *Step Five:* Use the knife blade to imprint lines on the large mushroom cap and the small mushroom stem. Use a toothpick to poke holes in the large stem and at the bottom of the small mushroom cap.

(FIGURE 25) Pinch off a small piece of dough and roll it between your fingers to form a ball, then slightly flatten the ball on one side. Dampen the flat side and place the ball on the smaller mushroom.

(FIGURE 26) Push a hairpin into the large mushroom cap to act as a hanger-upper for later. Prick the entire piece with a fine sewing needle.

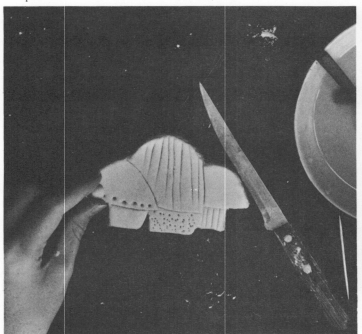

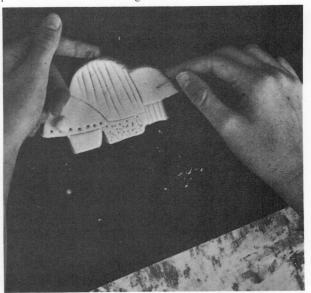

20

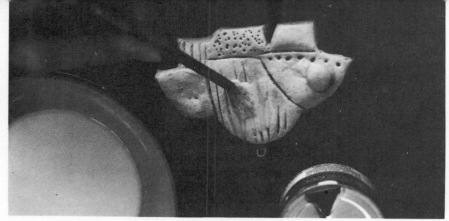

(FIGURE 27)   Bake for 1½ hours. Baste with canned evaporated milk during the last 30 minutes of baking. Remove from the oven and cool.

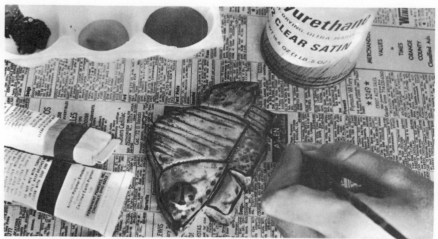

(FIGURE 28)   Use brown acrylic paint (slightly thinned with water) and a fine paintbrush to lightly paint the mushroom edges. Don't be puzzled over acrylic paints—look them up later in Chapter 10. For now, read and keep going. Paint the ladybug red and black. Let dry. Spray (outside, please) with clear resin or polyurethane varnish. Let dry. Turn the piece over and spray the back side. Let dry.

Hooray! You have actually made something out of Baker's Clay, a mushroom cluster like the one in Plate 2. Wasn't that easy? The other projects included in this chapter are every bit as simple to make as the mushroom cluster, and are also just as charming.

Brainstorming Idea

Use this very simple technique to make a wide variety of flat pendants or tree ornaments to keep or give away.

A Word about Shapes and Designs

Now that you've made a project, utilizing a simple shape, try your hand at a few more shapes, using the techniques you learned while making the mushrooms. Think for a minute of all the animal shapes you used to draw when you were a child—and if you're like me, you won't have to think hard because you haven't progressed much beyond Basic Cow, which is all the better anyhow. Drawing simplified animal shapes on Baker's Clay really isn't very difficult, and the finished pieces look charming hung on the wall separately or in a grouping. If you are wondering where to find a wide variety of other simple shapes and forms to use in a flattening project, try thumbing through children's books and scanning mod wrapping paper and unusual greeting cards from the stationery store. Keep your eyes open and look at attractive and unusual designs as you read magazine ads or product labels at the market. Best of all, *look* around at trees, acorns, leaves, vegetable and fruit shapes and weeds. Mother Nature (who doesn't fool around with basic designs) has created the best of all possible shapes and they have been around all the time, though you may not have been "tuned in" to looking for and at them. A good example of natural designs might be the lowly mushroom which turns up in all creative media. Once you have become hooked on looking for color, form, shape and design, you'll begin to collect more ideas for working with Baker's Clay than you can possibly ever use.

These framed chickens (see Fig. 29), entitled "The One That Got Away," are a good example of how a simple shape turned into one of my all-time Baker's Clay favorites. A friend of mine has farm-type wallpaper in her kitchen, featuring the most loveable and lumpy chickens I've ever seen. The background is black and white, like chicken wire. Every time I go into her kitchen, I drool over those darn chickens. One day I drew the basic shapes on a piece of scratch paper, then

Figure 29

set out to make myself some chickens to hang in my kitchen. Making the birds was easy: I cut the shapes out of flattened dough, used my trusty paper clip to make wing-like impressions, baked, then painted sparingly. In the back of my mind I could see the chickens mounted on a simple framed black and white board, so I scooted down to the fabric store to find some black and white fabric, but with no luck. Still, I was absolutely determined that the background was going to be black and white! So, settling down before a TV rerun, I hand-painted the blacklines onto a white board and it only took me three hours to do it.

(FIGURE 30) Simple 5-by-6-inch plaques make a good beginning project for children or adults. Practice imprinting designs or simple words on a piece of flattened cut-out dough, or simply bake a flat dough piece, then paint your slogan on it. Leather thong, used for hanging, is found at the shoe-repair shop or in the shoelace department of your supermarket.

The cow on page 112 was cut from one piece of flattened dough. A very simple outlining paint job gives a three-dimensional look to the legs. This technique of outline painting is simple to master and is one of the best ways to accent certain parts of Baker's Clay figures. The rest of the piece may be left natural.

Figure 30

Figure 32

(FIGURE 32) The school of fish are all the same basic shape, arranged to bake in slightly different poses. Notice that the eyes are large and buggy—a common feature of many Baker's Clay pieces of animals or children. The technique of making large eyes like these is simple enough for the smallest child to master. Pinch off a small piece of dough and fold it between your fingers, just as you did when making the ladybug shape to go on the mushroom cluster. Moisten the face area then place the ball in position. Make another ball, press it into place to form the other eye.

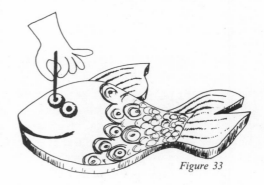

Figure 33

(FIGURE 33) Now take a toothpick or pencil with a sharp point and poke it into the center of the dough-ball, making the eye center. Create different expressions

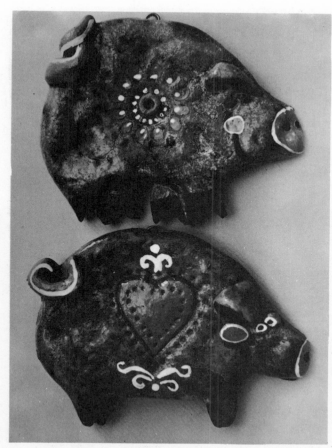

Figure 34

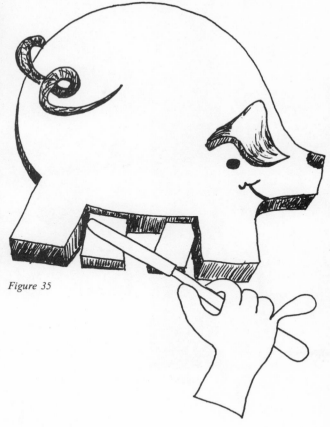

by poking through the doughball at different angles so that the eyes appear to be looking in different directions.

(FIGURE 34) "Two Pigs Out of a Poke" were basted every 30 minutes during their two hours in the oven to give them a dark brown color. One of my favorite imprinting tools is a small heart-shaped *hors d'oeuvre* cutter which was used to make the heart-shaped impressions on one of the pigs. After cutting out the pig shape, I used a knife tip to press the dough slightly flatter on the back legs so they would appear to be behind the front legs (see Fig. 35).

Figure 35

(FIGURE 36) What could be a more simple project that circular shapes, imprinted, basted and baked, then strung on a piece of leather thong?

(FIGURE 37) This rabbit is another example of what you can do with a simple animal shape. The piece was baked in a 200° oven for four hours, to keep the color light. The scroll painting was done directly on top of the light dough, and matte spray varnish was used to seal the piece without giving it any shine.

Figure 37

Figure 36

(FIGURE 38) I know you're thinking that angels are not supposed to be wearing shoes at all, much less Army-type combat boots. Let me explain what happened. The feet originally were small and looked more or less like feet are supposed to look. However, during baking, the feet puffed up and out of proportion, and needed only a paint job to transform them into boots.

26

Figure 38

Come to think of it, the history of mankind being what it is and has been, perhaps an angel shod this way is more appropriate than angels with petite bare feet.

You can incorporate twigs, branches, pods or cones with your Baker's Clay projects by simply pressing the pieces into the dough and baking as usual. Sometimes the dough will push away from wood or other substances during the baking process, but you can easily glue everything back together after the pieces have cooled. The "Key Caddy" (see Fig. 39) incorporates a medium-sized twig and some new elements—brass cuphooks. First screw the cup hooks into the wood; then press the wood into the dough slab, add bits and pieces of dough and pine cones and bake. Because Baker's Clay itself is an organic and natural craft medium, the addition of other natural materials blends in beautifully—which is why we have used so many straw flowers, weeds, pieces of scrap lumber and bark in projects scattered through the book. Besides, found materials don't cost anything—another good reason to use them

Figure 39

Figure 40

Figure 41

(FIGURE 40) This simply-shaped bird was placed on the cookie sheet, then the wings were cut apart from the body to bake separately. Easy-to-construct projects like this are simple to cut apart before baking. This makes the finished piece appear to be sophisticated and complicated when finally framed or mounted.

(FIGURE 41) For those of you who really enjoy painting iddy-biddy designs and intricate patterns, try a project like "Two Birds in a Bush." The bush was baked separately from the leaves and birds, everything was painted, then assembled and glued together inside the prepared frame. Depth was gained by placing one of the birds on top of the branch so it appears to be out in front of the bush.

(FIGURE 42) Here now is a masculine-appealing project you can easily give as a gift to dads, brothers, uncles, grandparents and male friends. The squares for this tic-tac-toe board were all cut separately, then moistened and joined before baking. Simple imprinting further defines the squares and basting during the last hour of baking will give the board a woody look. For added strength, glue a piece of thin, hard-surfaced particle board (from the lumber yard) to the back side just in case the board gets dropped, sat upon or carried off by the dog.

Brainstorming Idea

This project is ideal for kids because they all enjoy playing the game and the techniques of making the

Figure 42

board and cutting out the pieces are simple enough that the ultimate success of the project is guaranteed. Children in particular become distressed if their Baker's Clay pieces bubble in the oven, so be sure to use your sewing needle and prick all the surfaces thoroughly to eliminate most of the unsightly bubbles (besides, a lumpy tic-tac-toe board might be hard to use for a game.) You ambitious types may prefer to make a larger board to use for checkers or chess!

(FIGURE 43) This planter is a project which will require some measuring and the use of two cookie sheets so you can bake the whole thing at one time (see Fig. 44). First cut out the slabs and place them on the cookie sheets, then cut away sections to form the roofs and treetops. Do necessary imprinting and outlining to form windows and doors, then bake. The planter just happens to exactly fit around a plastic milk carton, which, with little alterations, makes a dandy planter box; not only is it waterproof, but it is also free. To prepare the milk carton, first push the end which opened to pour milk as flat as possible, holding it down with masking tape. Next, lay the carton flat on the table and cut a large hole on the top surface (see Fig. 45). Now proceed as if you were going to plant something. First add a layer of gravel, then sand, then planter mix and finally the plants. Seal the house pieces on all sides, then glue them together (but not to the milk carton). The house will be wobbly, so cut a piece of masonite or thin board 9 $\frac{1}{4}$ inches long by 4$\frac{1}{4}$ inches wide and glue it to the bottom of the piece, giving necessary support. Now you can lift the milk-carton planter in and out, or change it and substitute smaller clay pots if you wish. Use any type of container you desire to hold the plants. Look for small flat pots at the nursery or consider using those old casserole baking dishes with tops lost long ago that now are just taking up space in the cupboard. If you have a planter which is not particularly decorative, do some measuring and make a shape to go around it— you're not limited to house designs either—try castles, adobe missions, forts, trains, etc. If you give someone a Baker's Clay planter, caution them against getting the piece wet—and suggest that if they should accidentally douse it and somehow moisture seeps through the sealing, a disinfectant spray will kill the mold which will surely grow and will keep the piece from disintegrating totally.

If you look carefully at the planter box on the front

Figure 43

29

of one of the houses, you'll notice some straw flowers (from the hobby, variety or florist shop) which were inserted in the dough and baked along with the project. Bake flowers in the dough because it makes them become more a part of the project than when you glue them on later. Be careful when basting a piece that has straw flowers in it as the moisture in evaporated milk will make the flowers close tightly, never to open up again, so baste around them, never directly on top.

Figure 45

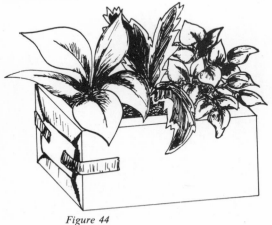

Figure 44

(FIGURE 46) Vegetable shapes are simple to make and look charming hanging on kitchen walls. Use your knife tip to imprint lines and give the shapes more definition. Onions never come flat at the market, but are always bunched tightly together. After cutting out three flat onions, I felt obligated to pick one up and place it on top of the other two for more authenticity.

Figure 46

About Patterns

Using paper patterns for cut-out shapes is a simple matter and will help you overcome a fear of making original designs at first. Start out using a pattern on a simple animal, mineral or vegetable shape like the mushrooms seen in Plate 2. By the time you graduate to something slightly more difficult, you most likely will have discovered that it's a snap to draw outlines directly on the flattened dough and you won't need to go to the bother of making a pattern.

Figure 47

(FIGURE 47) *Step One:* Lay a piece of tracing paper over the mushroom picture and draw it onto the paper.

(FIGURE 48) *Step Two:* Enlarge your tracing by copying the same exact lines, only drawing ¼ or ½ inch beyond the drawn lines (use a different color pen or pencil to make it easy to follow the new lines). Keep following this procedure making the drawing larger and larger until it is the size you want it to be.

Step Three: Cut out the drawing.

Step Four: Lay the cut-out pattern on top of the flattened dough and lightly draw around the edges, remove the pattern and cut the shape out. Now continue with imprinting, etc. and finish the mushrooms following the directions on page 19.

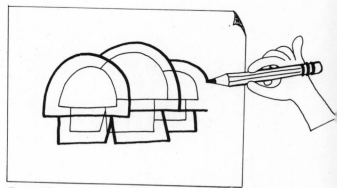

Figure 48

Brainstorming Idea

Often children's coloring books are filled with very simple shapes in good sizes for patterns to turn into Baker's Clay pieces. All you have to do is to cut the piece out of the coloring book, trace around it on the dough, and you're in business.

(FIGURE 49) Inspiration for these two pictures came from a soft-drink ad, which utilize the designs of sunbursts, planets, stars and simple landscape shapes. The simplicity of the shapes make this an easy project for you to draw on paper and enlarge to any size you want, following the same steps used in making the mushroom.

Some friends of mine were in charge of decorating a 6-foot-tall fir tree which was to be raffled off as part of a holiday fund-raising project for their good deed organization. Baker's Clay provided the perfect answer to making inexpensive, original ornaments, and cardboard patterns of the three shapes enabled the ladies

Figure 49

31

of varied creative skills to turn out several dozen identical gingerbreadlike pieces like the ones in Plate 1. The fine white outline on the pieces created the biggest headache, because the lines had to be uniform and straight and required a very steady hand and many hours of work if they were to be painted on. The answer to this problem came when one of the ladies decided to try putting thick latex house paint in her pastry sleeve, then used a tiny decorating tip to squeeze the paint through. Fortunately, she had lots of experience in decorating cakes and cookies, and in no time at all was able to put the white-line finishing touch on all the pieces.

An Alternative Method of Making a Pattern

Step One: Trace the drawing out of the book (just like you did with the other method).

Step Two: Use your ruler and a pencil to draw a perimeter (either square or rectangular) around the figure.

Step Three: Measure one side of the perimeter, then divide it into equal segments, like ½ or ¼-inch. Use these measurements and your ruler to draw lines across the drawing from top to bottom and side to side so that the drawing is now covered with equal-sized squares (see Fig. 50).

Step Four: Decide how big you want the piece to be when finished. Draw a new square or rectangle this size on a second piece of paper. Divide the top line into the same number of segments as the smaller drawing. Do the same on one side, then use your ruler and pencil to make squares like you did on the smaller drawing.

Step Five: Now copy, square by square, the lines from the smaller drawing (see Fig. 51). Use a pencil, so if you make a small mistake, you can erase it. After the drawing is complete, cut it out, lay it on a slab of dough and proceed as you did when making the mushroom

Molds and Other Shortcuts to Gorgeously Deceiving Baker's Clay

I know a lady who collects antique molds as a hobby and has a large variety of wooden and plaster replicas as well as cast-iron molds used for making cookies, novelty breads and fancy butter pats. She loaned me some molds to experiment with, and you can see the

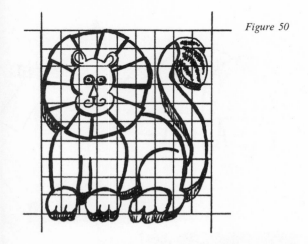

Figure 50

Figure 51

results of one of the projects. The figure from the mold is very intricate and was left unpainted, natural and trimmed as one variation, (see Fig. 52) and the other was sealed, then stained to resemble an old wood carving (see Fig. 53). Regardless of how you decide to finish the piece, the basics for working with all types of molds are exactly the same. First prepare the dough, then knead at least ¼ cup extra flour into it, making the dough feel very stiff. This is necessary as the dough must be hard so it will keep its shape once you take it out of the mold. Soft dough will puff up and the design will bake right out of it, destroying the object of using intricate molds to make unusual pieces.

Now that you have prepared a stiff batch of dough, turn your attention to preparing the mold. You are going to be pressing the dough into the mold, then removing it before you bake, and even stiff dough will not come out of any type of mold without help, which in this case comes in the form of cornstarch. Sprinkle cornstarch into the mold, then spread it evenly around using a soft, wide paintbrush (or pastry brush) (see Fig. 54). Pick the mold up and shake it over the sink to remove excess starch, then press and pat the dough into the mold. Keep patting until you have the mold full and lightly punch the dough all over so it fills all cracks and crevices (see Fig. 55). There is a trick in getting the dough out of the mold without flipping it all over the floor. Place your teflon cookie sheet right side down on top of the mold. Somehow, grab both the mold and the cookie sheet and flip them over at the same time. Now you have the mold, right-side-down on the cookie

Figure 52

Figure 53

Figure 54

Figure 55

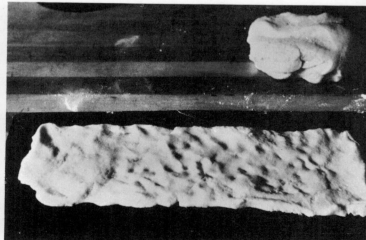

33

sheet (and not on the floor). Carefully lift up the mold just enough to get your fingers under one corner and pull at the dough until it starts to come out of the mold. This is all that is usually needed, as once the dough starts to separate from the mold it all pops out at once. Decide if you want to trim the excess dough away from the molded figure or not, and if you do, use a sharp knife for cutting the excess away so you don't pull the shape and discombuberate the whole thing. Use a very small sewing needle and carefully prick the whole piece so that it will bake as bubble-free as possible (again, preserving the design of the mold). If you use a shallow mold, the piece will be ½-inch or less thick. Thin pieces like this tend to crack and fall apart in the oven unless you turn the temperature down to 200° and check them carefully to remove as soon as they are dry throughout. Naturally, baking at this low temperature does not brown the pieces at all . . . but this can be remedied with a simple painting procedure covered in Chapter 10. Since the finished pieces often are very thin, they are bound to be very fragile. Brush a thick layer of white glue on the back side after you have completely finished painting, staining or sealing your project. This coat will give the piece the needed strength to withstand temperature changes and various jarring and flying objects.

Look for molds wherever hobby or kitchen supplies are sold. While most of these are designed for use with resin, wax or plaster, some are rather unusual and well suited for use with Baker's Clay. Baker's Clay picture frames made in small molds are absolutely beautiful and make very professional-appearing frames which you can use with a wide variety of pictures, especially those school pictures of children that make such nifty gifts for grandparents, aunts and uncles.

So what have you learned?

At this point you've learned what to put into Baker's Clay, how to knead it all together, how to flatten it out, how to cut out shapes, how to imprint and with what, how to layer some pieces, how to baste, how long to bake and always, always to seal.

You have also learned that:

* hairpins make dandy hanger-uppers for some projects and may be baked right in the dough;
* some pieces separate during baking but may be glued back together later;
* incurable baked-in lumps and bumps are to be loved and tolerated;
* pricking dough before baking often eliminates lumps and bumps;
* simple yet charming designs are easy to find once you get yourself tuned in to looking for them;
* funny round eyes are balls of dough, positioned, then poked with a toothpick;
* you can incorporate a whole raft of natural or scrounged materials with Baker's Clay projects;
* simple projects may be cut apart or separated during baking, then mounted with emphasis on the separation to make more complicated appearing projects;
* working with paper patterns is perfectly all right, even desirable in some cases;
* Baker's Clay may be used in a wide variety of molds.

FLATTENING II– 5
A LITTLE
HARDER

Now that you are familiar with the basic techniques of working with flattened dough, you can move on to more sophisticated procedures, still using the same basic flattening process.

To Cookie Cutter or Not to Cookie Cutter

At this point you must come to terms with a highly controversial matter, whether or not to rely on preconceived shapes provided by your nearby cookie cutters. In my opinion, the smooth geometric shapes provided by some cookie cutters are really terrific and make great Baker's Clay projects. If you feel timid about working with your own hand-drawn shapes at first, then by all means, use different-shaped cutters to give you a basic shape to embellish with dough trims of various shapes and sizes, then when you gain confidence in your own abilities, put the cookie cutters aside and move ahead on your own. Small children love to cut cookie cutter shapes out of flattened dough, and will spend hours doing so, wadding the shapes up and flattening the dough out over and over—only to wad the shape up, flatten it out and begin again. (We might, however, take a clue from little people. They soon tire of using the cutters, and if shown how to cut their own shapes out of the dough, will be able to do so quite easily.) My favorite cookie cutters are a set of variegated circle shapes, going from 1 inch in diameter to 3 inches in diameter, two different sizes of hearts (which when cut in half make terrific leaf shapes) and a couple of small *hors d'oeuvre* cutters.

Figure 58

"Baby Baubles" seen here (see Fig. 58) and in **Plate 7** illustrates the technique of using several different types of cutters to make layered framed pictures to hang on the Christmas tree or to place on wire in a potted plant as a gift for Grandma or Grandpa on Valentine's Day. Layering of many cut shapes, in this case to form designs, calls for working with dough rolled out to ¼-inch thickness. However, if layering causes the finished piece to be 1 inch thick or more, the problem of excessive bubbles will pop up (pardon the pun). The outside layer of dough cooks first, then the steam from lower layers wells up just under the top surface and causes bubbles and distortions. If you want the baubles to be flat like these, then prick the entire piece with a fine sewing needle before baking. As I explained before, these pinholes allow the steam to escape and the holes become almost invisible when the dough is thoroughly cooked. This handy trick is a good one to keep in mind on all projects you want to bake as flat as possible.

To make sure that you fully understand the principal steps of layering, make a few of the baubles to get the feel of working with thinner dough, cutting shapes out and layering them together.

(FIGURE 59) *Step One:* Gather a variety of geometric cutting tools. If you don't have easy access to cookie cutters, look around for empty glass jars, jar lids, pill containers, etc. Flatten the dough out to ¼-inch thickness.

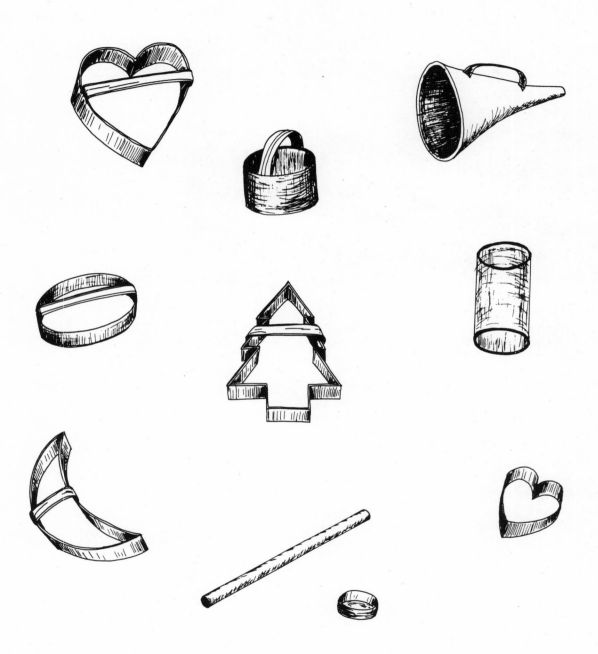

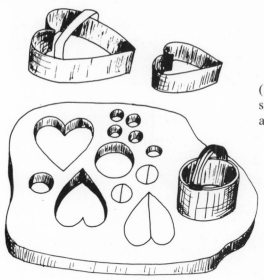

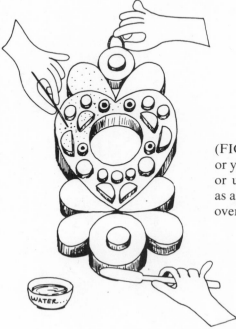

(FIGURE 60) *Step Two:* Begin by cutting either a heart shape or a circle to use as the back piece, then cut out additional shapes to place around it.

(FIGURE 61) *Step Three:* Moisten all pieces as you place them around and on top of the back piece. Cut a 1-inch circle from the center of the back piece.

(FIGURE 62) *Step Four:* Use a dampened knife blade or your finger to smooth all cut edges that may be rough or uneven. Insert a hairpin in the bauble top to serve as a hanger. Use a fine sewing needle and prick air holes over the entire surface.

Step Five: Bake at 300° for three hours or until done. If you desire a dark color, baste with evaporated milk during the last 1½ hours of baking time. If excessive bubbles appear, use your potholder and press all pieces as flat as possible, or bake with garden rocks on top. Remove from the oven and cool.

(FIGURE 63) *Step Six:* Paint, and seal with varnish.

(FIGURE 64) *Step Seven:* Trim the picture so that none of it shows beyond the border of the bauble.

Figure 63

Figure 64

(FIGURE 65) *Step Eight:* Rub glue around the opening on the back side on the bauble, then press the picture into place.

(FIGURE 66) *Step Nine:* Check the position of the picture from the front side to make sure that everything you want to show does so.

Figure 65

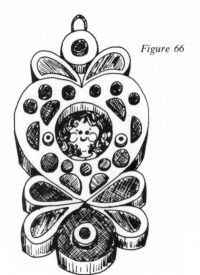

Figure 66

40

Step Ten: Cut a piece of brightly colored felt, large enough to cover the picture, and glue this onto the back side. This way the bauble looks good from both sides, which might not be too important if it's hanging on the wall, but might be very much so if it is hanging on a Christmas tree.

(FIGURE 67) You can modify geometric cut-out shapes and turn them into flowers and leaves to make wreaths like this and the colored one in Plate 3. First make the wide, flat leaves. Use a heart-shaped cookie cutter, cut out a heart, cut it in half and imprint leaf veins on it (Fig. 68). Next cut out the various flowers, dampen them on the back side and press into place. If you want the color to stay light, bake in a 250° oven for several hours. Or, if you wish, paint the wreath to give it a totally different look, even though the basic shapes are exactly the same.

Baker's Clay flowers (see Fig. 73) combined with a sheaf of wheat make for a beautiful and most unusual table centerpiece. Because the flowers are fairly heavy, you'll need to use coat-hanger wire for the stems. Cut the flowers out of ½-inch flattened dough and bake, making sure to poke a hole in the flower center large enough to receive a wire stem later. The dough will swell somewhat during baking, and you may have to repoke the holes as the flowers bake and dry. If you wish, paint the flowers, though these are absolutely handsome left the natural light color of the baked dough. Assembling is simple.

(FIGURE 69) *Step One:* Cut a length of coat-hanger wire. Bend a loop at one end and squeeze it tightly with your pliers or wire cutters.

(FIGURE 70) *Step Two:* Wrap the loop with dark brown florist's tape (from the hobby shop or floral supply shop).

Figure 67

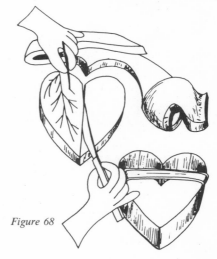

Figure 68

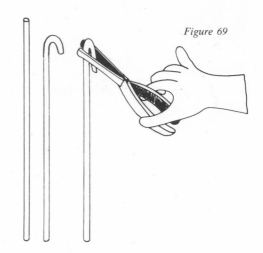

Figure 69

Figure 70

41

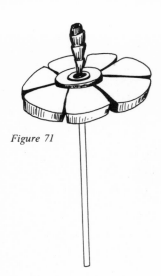

Figure 71

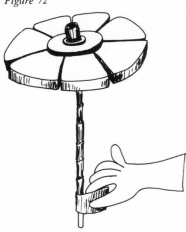

Figure 72

(FIGURE 71) *Step Three:* Push the wire through the flower center until the wrapped hook is touching the flower center. Place a glob of glue on the flower back side where the wire comes through the hole. Let dry.

(FIGURE 72) *Step Four:* Wrap the entire stem with florist's tape. Hold the wire stem and twist it around as you tape down the stem to the end.

Figure 73

(FIGURE 74) There are many interesting projects using strips of flattened dough which you can easily bake up. For instance, some of these words could be made for a favorite, harried (or bald) advertising executive. If you want your words to stand up after they are

42

Figure 74

baked, prop them against the edges of your cookie sheet so that they will bake with a flat bottom edge (see Fig. 75). First flatten a batch of dough to ½-inch thickness, then cut strips 1-inch wide. Use these to form the words and be sure to moisten the dough where it touches itself by dabbing these places with a wet paint brush. If some of the letters separate during baking, you can glue them back together later. Baste the letters three times during the last hour of cooking so they will become dark and woodlike.

Figure 75

Brainstorming Idea

Try making placecards or words for different seasons or occasions (see Fig. 76).

Figure 76

You might decide to bake words or slogans directly on a piece of interesting wood, so do yourself and your oven a favor by placing some foil under the wood just in case it starts to leak sap onto the bottom of your oven.

Breadbaskets and other woven containers (see Fig. 77) offer a novel way of using flat strips of Baker's Clay, and they are very easy to do. First select the container you will be using to weave the dough strips over to give them shape; in this case it was a loaf pan. Cover the pan with aluminum foil. Cut a goodly supply of dough strips ½-inch thick and 1-inch wide, then begin to lattice them on top of the covered pan—just like weaving the dough top of a cherry pie. You can use any type of container to give a Baker's Clay basket shape, as long as the container is ovenproof. Bake two to five hours at 250°, cool, then slide the basket off the foil and spray it thoroughly with varnish. You might just as well whip up some napkin rings to go with the basket. Cut some smaller strips, weave them in a small circle to bake, or weave them around a covered straight glass.

Figure 77   Figure 78

(FIGURE 78) Flattened strips were used to make the different length sun rays on "Ol Sol." Very thin strips, cut ¼-inch wide were used to outline eyes, nose, and mouth.

(FIGURE 79) Speaking of suns, try creating a variety of different small sun faces (no larger than 6 inches across), then mounting them on rough scraps of unfinished lumber.

Did you know that your dearly-beloved garlic press is good for much more than squashing buds to flavor spaghetti sauce? Stringlike clumps of Baker's Clay, used to make grass or hair, are made by pushing small wads of dough through the press, then placing them in position on the cut-out shape. To make extra long pieces of grass (or hair) push a wad of dough through the press, and lay it carefully on the cutting board while you refill it with a second wad of dough. Press this through and continue filling the press until the strings are as long as you want them to be. Small pieces like this (see Fig. 80) which are designed to hang alone or unmounted on the wall can be rather fragile. Remedy this by smearing a thick layer of white glue on the back side of the piece when it comes out of the oven. Smear a layer of glue thickly on all pieces which need extra strength.

Figure 79

Figure 81

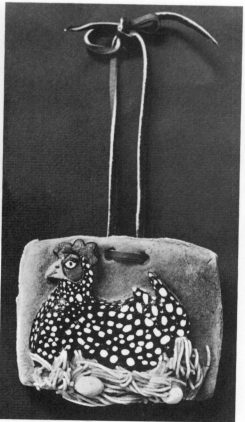

(FIGURE 81) For those of you who really like to work on itty-bitty things, try arranging the garlic press strings one at a time into intricate designs as was done on the turtle's shell. The dough strings are very soft and squishy right after they come out of the press; however, if you let them sit on the breadboard for five minutes (any longer, and the pieces will become too brittle to use) you'll find they are slightly dry and easier to arrange into various types of designs.

45

Figure 80

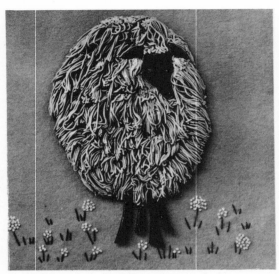

Figure 82.

(FIGURE 82) This lamb will give you lots of practice with the press—his entire body is a mass of garlic-pressed dough strings. You'll need about ¼ batch of dough to make a nice full and round lamb body, and very little flattened dough to cut face and legs.

"Victorian Villa" seen in **Plate 9** is a project which uses all the flattening and layered techniques you have learned so far. Thin strips of cut dough form part of the door and general house outline, window designs were cut into the dough with a sharp knife tip, and flattened pea-sized balls layered over each other make roof shingles.

(FIGURE 83) The "Car-Pool Queen" and Other Clever Cookies—to be taken in any way you wish! When we were brainstorming and planning the projects for this book, it occurred to us that we needed medals, plaques or other commemorative memorabilia to give to ourselves or other deserving persons exemplifying some activity or another at which we excelled (not always by choice). The "Car-Pool Queen" was originally intended to be a small pin, but as often happens, the piece became larger and larger, and unless you have a wide lapel or size Double-D chest, would fit better hanging on the wall beside the car keys, near the front door, or on gold cord from the rear-view mirror in your taxi (otherwise known as the family car). The words were cut out of dough flattened to ¼-inch in diameter, and poked into place with a toothpick, which also left an interesting imprinted design (sometimes those mistakes turn out to be the best thing about the project). The "Good Guy" award might be a lighthearted way of saying thanks to the school principal or a favorite teacher at the end of the school year.

Figure 83

(FIGURE 84) "Christmas Mouse," hungrily clutching his hunk of cheese, was designed by my daughter, who had drawn the creature in a fifth-grade art class. Trying to keep the finished piece as much like her drawing wasn't too difficult, as I first traced around her mouse, then enlarged it somewhat using the method described on page 31. The whiskers are pieces of hairpins, cut, then pushed into the dough before baking. When making this piece I wasn't very experienced with Baker's Clay and didn't know that long or extended pieces of dough are quite fragile and need to have a piece of wire inserted into them before baking to prevent breakage (see Fig. 85). Any time you are working on a project with thin or extending pieces, save yourself grief over fractures by pushing wire bits into areas that need extra strength.

Figure 84

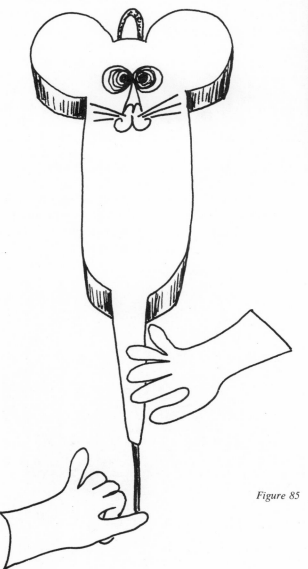

Figure 85

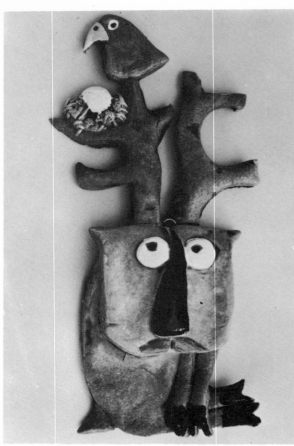

Figure 86

Positioning Cut Dough Shapes

(FIGURE 86) There will be times when you will want to make a simple cut-out shape without too much fussing, but would like to give the project a little extra zing without taking much time: try positioning the cut-out shape. First, cut out the basic shape—in this case the reindeer body which is one piece, then cut out a second piece, the head and antlers. Place the body on your cookie sheet and carefully lift the front legs to fit over the hind legs, creating a somewhat sitting position (see Fig. 87). Next position the head and antlers on top of the body, then add the features, garlic pressed bird's nest and the simple bird shape. Be sure to dampen the dough where it overlaps or touches itself so that the pieces bake together and don't pop out of place.

Figure 87

Another example of positioning cut-out shapes is "Little Folks" wall plaques on page 137. The basic shapes of all the children are exactly the same (see Fig. 88). First use a knife tip to outline the entire figure, then cut it out and place on your cookie sheet. Cut out any extra shapes like the rabbit, place in position, then fold arms and legs or whatevers to hold the objects or make the figure appear to be doing what you want it to be doing. Last of all, add garlic-pressed hair.

Baker's Clay can provide the perfect answer to the problem of seasonal centerpieces for home or luncheon meetings. Even the most simple forms can be baked with a piece of wire in the center (see Figs. 89, 90, 91, 92, 93, 94 and 95).

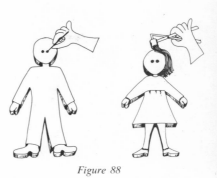

Figure 88

Figure 89

Figure 90

Figure 91

Figure 92

Figure 93

Figure 94

Figure 95

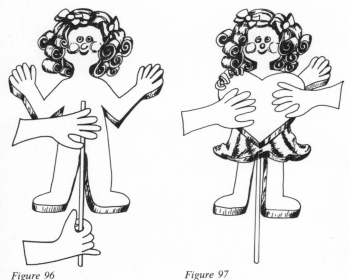

Figure 96   *Figure 97*

Figure 98

(FIGURE 96) First cut out the basic shape and place it on your cookie sheet, then press the piece of cut coat hanger wire into the dough.

(FIGURE 97) Second, add embellishments to cover the wire, then bake as usual or you might wish to substitute wooden doweling for the wire. If you want the finished piece to stand up in a block of wood, as opposed to being used to perk up a house plant, use coat-hanger wire cut long enough so you have 1 inch left over and protruding from the bottom of the piece. After all is baked and painted, put this inch of wire into a block of wood to make your project a free-standing piece of sculpture. Some of these pieces look best mounted over rough scrap lumber or even driftwood. You'll find more ideas on various types of mounting materials in Chapter 10.

(FIGURE 98) If the man or boy in your life is in need of a special award for effort, make him a Baker's Clay trophy commemorating his achievement.

Simple Baker's Clay shapes make unusual backings to hold small mirrors (see Fig. 99). You can find small, inexpensive mirrors at the dime or drugstore, or can pull them out of old compacts. If the mirrors are small, you needn't worry about the normal distortion of cheapies, since most folks will be looking at the total piece and not particularly at themselves in the mirror. Baking mirrors with Baker's Clay usually ends up disastrously. If the mirror doesn't shatter when exposed to all that heat, it will become destroyed when the moisture from the dough wells up beneath it and boils off the mirror backing. So, cut out the shape, embellish it, put in the hairpin hanger, prick all over with pinholes, then push the mirror into the place you want it to be, just to make sure you have left enough room for it, and then remove the mirror and pop the piece in your oven. Continue checking the piece as it bakes, because you will really need the area where the mirror will be glued to be as flat as possible. If air bubbles form there, push them down with a potholder or re-prick with more pin holes. After the piece is painted and sealed, glue the mirror into place.

When gluing mirrors onto anything, you always run the risk of the glue's seeping through to the front, causing brown grainy distortions to appear on the mirror. To prevent this, cut a piece of self-adhesive vinyl paper the same size as the mirror, and stick this to the back, then glue the mirror onto the Baker's Clay shape. Self-adhesive paper is waterproof and while it holds onto

50

the mirror tightly, it also keeps the glue from seeping through to the mirror backing.

(FIGURE 100) If you prefer, measure the diameter of the mirror, create the shape you wish to hold the mirror, then cut a hole in the center of the piece, trimming it slightly smaller than the mirror diameter. After baking, painting and sealing, glue the mirror in back of the hole.

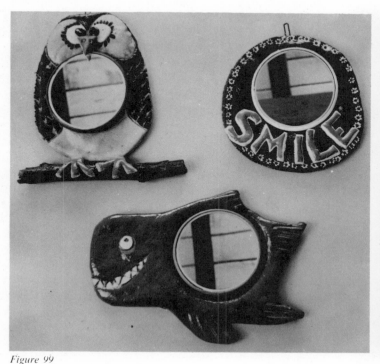

Figure 99

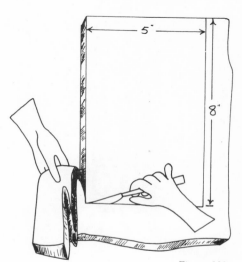

Figure 100

On Being Practical

Should you be one of those who feel that handcrafted projects must be useful, functional Baker's Clay holders like the one seen in Plate 4 should be for you. One-half inch flattened dough can be made into flower holders, weed pots, pencil containers and letter baskets (to give those pesky bills a place to abide til payday). The secret to keeping portions of Baker's Clay things open until they are baked is to use kitchen aluminum foil as support; you remove the foil after the project is finished.

(FIGURE 101) Begin by cutting a slab of flattened dough, making it slightly larger than the things which you plan on putting in it. This letter holder, back piece, for example, is 5 inches wide and 8 inches long.

51

Figure 101

Figure 102

Figure 103

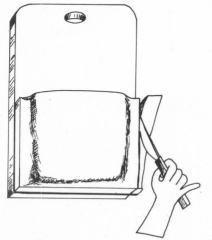

Figure 104

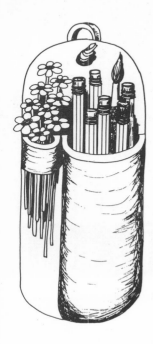

Figure 105

(FIGURE 102) Place the slab on your cookie sheet, then wad up some foil to form a smooth, flattish shape, a square, rectangle or oblong or what-have-you to hold up the next piece of dough.

(FIGURE 103) Cut your next piece of dough as long as you wish it to be, and slightly larger than the bottom piece (which you have cut already). Drape this second piece over the foil, moisten where the dough touches, then press three edges together (leaving the top open).

(FIGURE 104) If you have miscalculated, and the top piece is more than slightly larger than the back piece, just cut away the excess. If, however, it is too small, pull it off the foil and cut a second piece, then try again. Be sure to poke holes in the top to hold thong, string or yarn for hanging later on, then pop the piece in the oven.

Having a hunk of foil inside Baker's Clay changes the baking time considerably, because the moisture can't get through the foil, just plan on baking the piece longer. Since overbaking makes Baker's Clay very brittle, turn the oven to 250° and allow the piece to bake for 4 or 5 hours. After that, the top and bottom hunks of dough should be solid and dry, so use kitchen tongs and pull the foil out of the middle, allowing the heat to get to the center part and speed up the baking time. Just make sure that the top piece is good and solid and not mushy and soft, because once you remove the support, it will cave in. As always, be 150% positive that the whole piece is done before you stop baking. You'll notice a large crack running down the front section of the letter holder, and if you look very closely you'll see that it runs through the face (even though I tried to camouflage it with a second coat of paint). This crack serves to underscore the importance of baking pieces until they are thoroughly dry. Several months after the letter holder had been finished and hung on the wall, it fell apart, plunk! During my postmortem examination, I discovered some spots of penicillin (mold) growing on the inside of the front section which also explained that funny odor in the kitchen. The holder was not damaged beyond the point of a glue-job repair, so I sprayed all pieces with Lysol (to kill the mold), glued everything back together, then rebaked it in a 200° oven for two hours. Now the holder lives happily ever after.

By simply altering the basic shapes of the hanging holders, you can make receptacles to hold weeds, tall thin floral arrangements, pencils, or paper clips (Fig. 105).

Be sure to "fix" all dried weeds, etc. by spraying with a thorough coat of hair spray (which is fine quality lacquer). This seals everything, kills bugs and keeps shredding to a minimum.

When that end-of-school-year, Grandpa's birthday or scout leader's internment rolls around, weed pots are a good project for children to undertake. Insure long life for all holders by smearing glue on the back and inside.

Smaller flower holders, like these pieces called "Women's Lib and Friend" (see Fig. 106) also require small pieces of foil inserted in areas or places which are intended to hold flowers or weeds later on. Fingers on Baker's Clay people look difficult yet are very easy to make if you have a pair of fingernail scissors lying around the house. After the piece is cut out and positioned, pick up a hand and snip it to cut out five fingers, then reposition to bake (see Fig. 107).

Figure 105

Figure 107

Figure 106

53

The little figure with the crack running through her face serves as a good example of mistakes which should not only be tolerated, but should also be enjoyed and occasionally discussed. We have a 20-pound cat who would rather steal Baker's Clay and lick it to oblivion than go after mice or other garage residents. The flower holder had just come from the oven and was cooling on the table when the cat leaped up, grabbed it and ran off to hide and enjoy the illegally gained snack. After much chasing and threatening, I managed to catch him and get the piece out of his clutches, only to find that in the chase, the head of the figure had been badly cracked: in fact, it was only being held together by the hairpin which was inserted to be the hanger. At first I was distressed by the damage and considered catching the aforementioned beast and turning him into a rug or a purse, but after a moment, decided that the crack actually gave the figure sort of an irritated look (much like mine at the time), so I painted and sealed it. Now it's my favorite.

(FIGURE 108) Make a novel wall hanging by outlining your (or your children's hands) on dough, shaping the fingers to hold flowers after baking. Be sure to remember to place some foil in the space where the flowers will ultimately go. This project is a welcome change from the plaster of paris hands that children make in kindergarten or first grade.

About Shapes and Shaping

There are limitless possibilities of things which you can put in or under Baker's Clay to help give it shape while baking—and here is just a partial list:

Empty Pop or Beer Cans

(FIGURE 109) This project, called "Canned Cow" got its shape by being baked over an empty aluminum pop can. You have to squash the can slightly so one side is a little flat and won't roll all over the cookie sheet (see Fig. 110). Arrange ½-inch flattened piece of dough over the can, cutting away to form legs or what-have-yous. Bake a flat head separately, and after the pieces are cooled, paint and glue them together. Using this technique, you can make a whole herd of four-legged animals—creating beasts like goats, horses, dogs, cats, elephants etc.

Figure 109

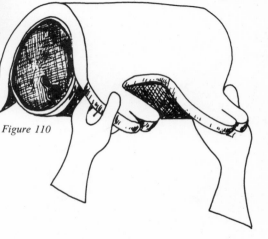

Figure 110

Figure 111

Walnut Shells

(FIGURE 111)   These small pieces were baked directly over walnut-half shells, which are still inside.

Newspaper Wads and Toilet Paper Roll Cores

(FIGURE 112)   The free-form shape of this hanging weed pot is made by first wadding up some newspapers to form an uneven ball, squashing the paper onto the cookie sheet and draping the flattened dough over the paper. Trim away the dough to get the shape you particularly like, then add the sleeves to hold weeds or flowers. Roll the dough around the paper cores and lay them in position, being sure to moisten all touching surfaces. This particular piece is really dark brown, in fact, even feels like leather because of constant basting every 20 minutes during baking.

Figure 112

56

Bowls and Dishes

Your kitchen cupboard might be full of ovenproof dishes which are great to use to give nice rounded shapes to Baker's Clay pieces. Two words of warning:

(1) Make sure that the piece you are going to use is ovenproof before you place it in the oven under a Baker's Clay project.

(2) Either spray the kitchen piece with a nonstick cooking spray, or cover it with aluminum foil, unless of course, you want it to be with the Baker's Clay project forever.

A kitchen fork was used to imprint around the edges of the sun face seen in Plate 5 to help give it that pottery look, and the simple features were cut out of flattened dough. The face was basted every 30 minutes during its two hours of baking time to make it dark. It sits on a block of scrap lumber, but could be hung on the wall.

(FIGURE 113) "Anyone for an Omelet?" A small kitchen bowl was placed under the center of this chicken's tummy, and the cooking pot was fashioned out of flattened dough, then placed flat on the cookie sheet in such a position that it looks as though it's under the chicken. All the "feathers" are made by pressing a bent paper clip into the dough.

Figure 113

Figure 114

Empty Bottles

(FIGURE 114) Patting or wrapping flattened dough around shapes can be both rewarding and frustrating, because occasionally the dough decides to do its own thing, which may be to slide off the container completely. You can turn empty aspirin, spice, jelly or other small bottles into charming pencil holders or weed pots by wrapping dough around the container, then decorating it with small dough snippets. Gently pat the dough completely around the bottle, then use your kitchen knife to cut away the excess (see Fig. 115). Be sure you moisten all overlapping and touching dough edges. You've probably been throwing away lots of small glass jars and bottles (see Fig. 116). Salvage them and turn them into charming weed pots like these. Be sure to include your children in this project. Little fing-

Figure 115

Figure 116

ers particularly love to pat and push dough around small containers.

(FIGURE 117) Turn a glass bottle or jar over and you have a base upon which to build a zoo or lumpy, squat creature similar to "Irwin Owl." Don't start by putting feathers or whatevers directly on the bottle; first pat the dough to cover the container as you did when covering bottles, then add embellishments to define the creature you happen to be making. If the dough ends up being layered quite heavily in any one area, be sure to prick it thoroughly with a pin.

Figure 117

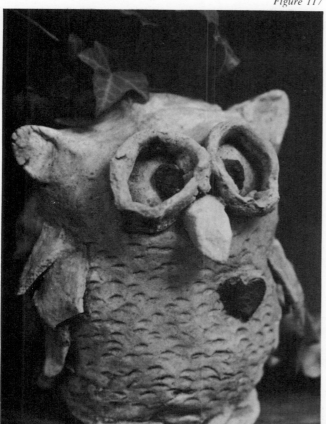

So what have you learned?

Before marching onwards and upwards to Flattening III, take stock of some steps which you've mastered in Flattening II . . . things like:

* cookie cutters are fun to use on certain types of projects;
* thick dough pieces won't bubble excessively if you prick them with a sewing needle to allow trapped air to escape;
* smearing white glue on the backs of finished projects will give them more strength and longer life;
* flattened dough can be cut in strips and turned into words or slogans;
* the lowly garlic press makes marvelous hair, straw and grass;
* simple cut-out shapes can be made to look more complicated or sophisticated if you position the arms and legs;
* table centerpieces or plant perk-ups will stand up if you bake a wire support in the center;
* don't bake mirrors and Baker's Clay together;
* you can bake all sorts of household junk into or under Baker's Clay to make things with unusual shapes;
* Baker's Clay projects can result in useful and practical items;
* tolerate cracks and other imperfections caused by human or non-human errors;
* underbaked projects will become moldy, but this can be cured and repaired;
* wrapping flattened dough around different shaped bottles is fun to do.

6 FLATTENING III— HARDER STILL

There may come a time in your development as a Baker's Clay crafter when you will want to tackle a project that, when finished and assembled, could be mistaken more for an *objet d'art* than something you popped into the oven.

I know, I know, you're grumbling to yourself that even though you appreciate unusual pieces of art and sculpture (and who doesn't?) you don't have the ability to copy a picture or a drawing of some arty piece, can't pull arty ideas out of your head and really can't make anything more basic than mushrooms or sun faces. For the moment, I'll agree with you, at least partially. Mastery of Baker's Clay doesn't start with a complicated project. After you have mixed up several batches of dough and have created some weed pots, centerpieces and other things, you'll have a feeling for the medium. You will know when the dough has been kneaded enough, will have some understanding of how to achieve the finish you want, and you'll be ready to tackle Baker's Clay pieces made to resemble actual art objects. Your local museum or library is stocked with books on art, painting and sculpture covering styles that range from Greek frescoes to sketches by Peter Max. Start *looking* through magazines and books for pictures or ideas which interest you. As you wander through your department or furniture store, *look* at the accessory pieces, regardless of whether they are made of wood, straw, plastic or pottery. Even if you can't draw a straight line (like me), before long you'll be taking a pad and pencil with you everywhere to sketch something which you've seen worth duplicating in Baker's Clay.

My "Christmas Colossus" in Plate 11 (or "the behe-

61

moth" as my husband calls it), is a good example of taking the basic flattening pieces as far as you can go and then some. Even though the dimensions of this piece are 5½ by 3½ feet, the techniques involved don't go beyond simple flattening, imprinting and layering. Original plans for the picture called for a simple manger scene with one or two buildings, a couple of angels and a lamb or two. But as often happens, one building led to another, then another, two angels became four, one piece needed another to balance it on the other side, as it turned into a family project with the kids busily cutting out people, painting the building surfaces and helping to glue the pieces in place. This is a big piece, I know, and you may be reluctant to try it, unless you are a Christmas nut like me. On the other hand, if you have some self-control and can stop after making just a few angels and buildings, you can keep the size down to where you can handle it easily. The project was included in this book after I discovered quite by accident that more than one person can work on a large Baker's Clay undertaking, and if someone supervises the whole operation the parts of the finished project will more or less blend together rather well.

If you are a teacher, or are involved with a group of youngsters, consider having your whole gang undertake a large Baker's Clay wall piece. You can vary the subject matter to cover whatever you happen to be studying at the time. This gives you two-for-the-price-of-one. The children will learn to work in a new and inexpensive art medium, and will enjoy making this type of a wall mural as opposed to the usual which is painted or done with crayons. As for Sunday School teachers, this type of a mural is ideal for your classes to work on before the Easter or Christmas holidays. Other subject matter which would work beautifully into a large Baker's Clay group project would be a transportation study, Indian pueblos, geography studies, farm animals, the evolution of man, the ecological balance, plant growth, city planning, and western towns.

If the thought of trying to engineer a frame for a wall project done by a whole group gives you a migraine, forget about framing. All classrooms have bulletin boards, so have the children insert hairpin hangers into their pieces, arrange them as desired by pinning the pieces onto the bulletin board, and when you are finished with the study, let the children take their own pieces home to hang in their rooms.

62

Figure 119

(FIGURE 119) I particularly like to mount or frame Baker's Clay on stained wood; the two materials compliment one another, and as you can see here, basted Baker's Clay, done in flower form, then glued onto wood, gives the appearance of carved wood.

Step One: Roll the dough to ⅛ or 3/16 inches in thickness. Cut several dough triangles, then roll one triangle to form the center (see Fig. 120).

Step Two: Carefully add remaining petal shapes to make the flower as full as you want it to be (see Fig. 121). Make several flowers and buds and set aside for a minute while you make the leaves.

Step Three: Cut leaf shapes and press in vein lines (see Fig. 122). Crimp the leaf along the center, then fold back to give a natural curve. If you want leaves with lots of shape, bake them supported by small wads of foil.

Make sure that all touching surfaces are dampened first, and that everything touches something so the piece will bake together. Baste during the last hour with evaporated milk (or longer if you want the finished pieces to be darker than these). Seal before you glue them onto the stained and sealed box or wood block. These projects are among the most unusual I have seen utilizing Baker's Clay and natural colored wood. They make particularly good projects to sell at bazaars or boutiques—one group made up several as samples, then took orders for fifty-five during an afternoon benefit sale.

Brainstorming Idea

Jazz up the appearance of inexpensive, store-purchased picture frames using this technique. Measure

Figure 120

Figure 121

Figure 122

63

Figure 123

Figure 124

the frame, then make the flowers to fit it exactly. Or think big and make a large floral arrangement to mount over an uninteresting inside door.

It is possible to work directly on the piece of wood you intend to use in mounting the finished project. When you plan to use materials like pods, cones, dried weeds or other scrounged materials, you can just push these things into place in the dough and bake everything together. The natural color and feeling of Baker's Clay blends beautifully with found things like pods and cones (see Fig. 123). Twigs, branches, rocks, etc. can be popped into the oven and baked as long as the oven temperature never exceeds 300° (any higher and the materials become so dry that they fall apart in a few weeks). *Heed this:* If your plan includes gluing scrounged materials onto the piece instead of baking them with it, be sure to eliminate bugs and other wee creatures from the materials first. Avoid the embarrassment of having your project sprout all sorts of interesting vermin by baking the scrounged materials in a preheated 300° oven for three or four hours. This simply and gently annihilates any wee beasties making their home in the materials.

A case in point involves my first project with Baker's Clay pods and cones. I created a candle ring utilizing Baker's Clay fruit shapes tucked in amongst pods and cones, but I didn't bake the pods or cones with the dough, instead glued them in place after the baking was finished. I gave this piece to my aunt at Christmas time, and she graciously placed the arrangement upon her prized grand piano, then left for a two-week vacation. She discovered, upon her return, that the arrangement, prized piano and all wood furniture in the room were infested with termites. Possessing a practical mind and forgiving nature, she fumigated her piano and other furniture, then suggested in the future that I dispose of the natural creatures before giving away the natural projects. So, unless alienating relatives appeals to you, make sure you bake all pods, cones and natural materials separately if you don't bake them with the project.

Large, slablike projects are easy to make and look terrific hanging around the house, but they do present one problem which we have not been able to solve, and have so merely tolerated (see Fig. 124). Extra-thick or slab pieces of Baker's Clay almost always crack while baking or do so shortly after removal from the oven, even after pricking them with a goodly number of air holes. For some reason, Baker's Clay cannot take the stress or heat

64

or humidity or something, so it cracks, similar in theory to what causes earthquakes I guess. If you can psyche yourself into an attitude of considering cracking to be like the weather, tolerated, but not entirely understood, then you won't mind when it happens. I have also learned, the hard way as usual, that heavy slab projects need quite a bit of support; a piece of masonite, cut smaller than the piece and glued to the back, is ideal. Adequate support sometimes will keep large flat pieces from cracking, and so will a good, thick layer of white glue smeared onto the back of the piece.

Unrepaired cracks, like the one in the middle of the toucan bird piece (see Fig. 125) will continue to grow until the piece falls apart. A never-fail cure for cracks is to fill them with thick craft glue. After the glue has dried, brush a smooth layer over the entire front area, dry and then repaint (see Fig. 126). Prevent the crack from reappearing by gluing a piece of masonite or thin wood to the back (as you should have done in the first place). To be forewarned, in this case, won't guarantee that nothing will happen, it merely tells you how to deal with the situation

Figure 125   *Figure 126*

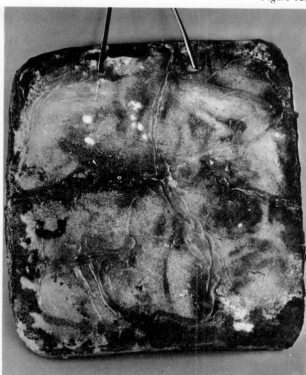

My husband and I are interested in ancient South American temple ruins, but aside from some framed photographs of art pieces dating back to those times, have little to show for our interest. "Mother and Child" seen in Plate 13 was made from ½-inch flattened dough pieces and fashioned as shown in one of our photographs. The dough cracked magnificently down the front, and although this did create the need for a second paint job, it made the figures look more like they dated back to Pre-Columbian than to predinner days.

"Knights and Castles" in Plate 6 may appear to be a complicated project, yet really is not. If you study it for a moment, you'll see that the horses and riders are all the same basic shape, arranged to bake in different positions. If your thing is medieval goings-on, then this type of project is for you. Other themes which could be carried out likewise are cowboys and Indians, or cavemen and dinosaurs.

Maybe you have been intrigued by those gingerbread houses perpetually featured in the make-it, bake-it magazines issued during the holidays. Or perhaps you have wanted some very special baked centerpiece to use for children's parties or to really deck out the table during a special occasion dinner or buffet party. "Gingerclay House" (see Fig. 127) is basically very simple to make, although there are many steps, which make it a reasonably time-consuming project. The project, much like "Christmas Colossus," started out to be simple, but as often happens, one shape led to another, one assembling technique led to another, and the project, like Jack's beanstalk, just grew and grew.

Figure 127

A Word About Coloring the Dough

Look at the project on the cover and notice how the dough takes on different shades of brown, yet doesn't appear to be painted. There are several substances which you can add to Baker's Clay dough to give it different colors, and these will be discussed further in Chapter 10. For now, all you need to do is scrounge up some instant coffee. Mix up a batch of dough to make the walls and roof, but first dissolve ½-cup instant coffee in the water before you put everything together. Another change in the dough, besides its new color, will be a new aroma—almost good enough to eat! Set this dough aside in a plastic sack and mix up a second batch, this time using only ⅛-cup of coffee, then mix up a third batch of dough, adding no coffee at all. The house doesn't use this much dough, so you'll have leftovers to use on something else.

Start by working on one wall at a time and find the flattest, most sturdy cookie sheet to bake the piece on. Crummy el-cheapo cookie sheets will often pop or warp in the oven. My broiler pan is very heavy and flat on the bottom. When a project calls for pieces that are large and perfectly flat, I turn the pan upside down, place a piece of foil over it, and use this as a baking sheet.

When you are making a project which requires rather precise shaping of separate pieces, you should first make paper patterns for the pieces that have to fit together after baking. So, make paper patterns for the house side, front and end pieces and the roof (see Fig. 128). Next roll out the dough which is darkest in color, cut a slab 6 by 10 inches and place this on your cookie sheet or sturdy baking pan. Place the pattern over the slab to double check that the dough is precisely the right size. Cut two pieces 2 by 4 inches to make the windows, place in position, then cut pieces of lighter-colored dough to make the window frames. Once you have the windows in place, begin to cut small, thin strips of flattened dough, using all three colors as shown, to make the squiggly designs on the remaining wall surface. Add a few bricks here and there, then the circles. Find something small and round, like the tip end of a pastry decorating set. Use this to cut many small circles out of the different colors of dough. As you place the circles in position, imprint them in the center using the other end of the pastry tip. Prick the piece with a sewing needle, then bake approximately 3 or 4 hours, checking it constantly for signs of warping. Repeat this procedure to make the other side and two end pieces.

67

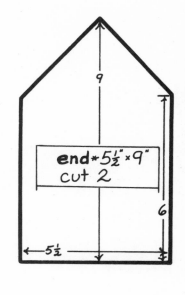

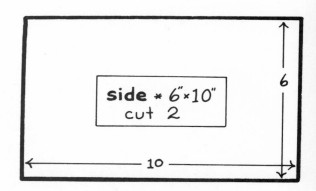

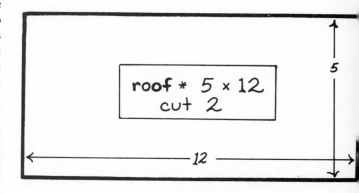

Figure 128

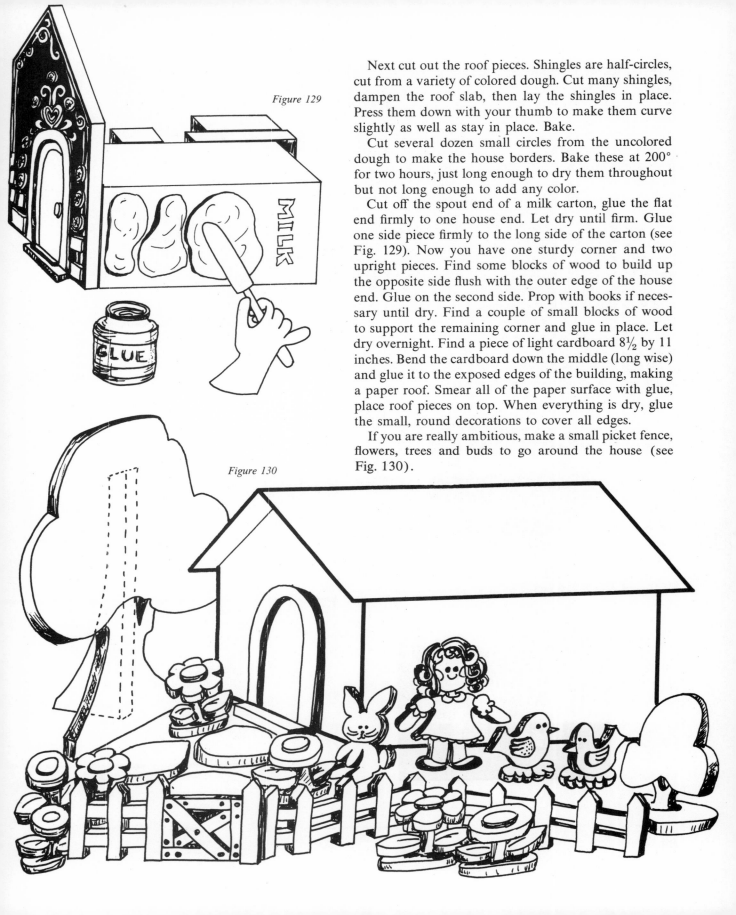

Figure 129

Next cut out the roof pieces. Shingles are half-circles, cut from a variety of colored dough. Cut many shingles, dampen the roof slab, then lay the shingles in place. Press them down with your thumb to make them curve slightly as well as stay in place. Bake.

Cut several dozen small circles from the uncolored dough to make the house borders. Bake these at 200° for two hours, just long enough to dry them throughout but not long enough to add any color.

Cut off the spout end of a milk carton, glue the flat end firmly to one house end. Let dry until firm. Glue one side piece firmly to the long side of the carton (see Fig. 129). Now you have one sturdy corner and two upright pieces. Find some blocks of wood to build up the opposite side flush with the outer edge of the house end. Glue on the second side. Prop with books if necessary until dry. Find a couple of small blocks of wood to support the remaining corner and glue in place. Let dry overnight. Find a piece of light cardboard 8½ by 11 inches. Bend the cardboard down the middle (long wise) and glue it to the exposed edges of the building, making a paper roof. Smear all of the paper surface with glue, place roof pieces on top. When everything is dry, glue the small, round decorations to cover all edges.

If you are really ambitious, make a small picket fence, flowers, trees and buds to go around the house (see Fig. 130).

Figure 130

(FIGURE 131) "The Bird Woman" is one piece I'm particularly fond of, and it has begat many similar pieces which I've given to relatives and friends. Inspiration for this piece came from an Egyptian tomb painting which I have always admired since clipping it out of a National Geographic magazine years ago. The painting was of a woman with a very elongated neck, holding an animal. The piece wouldn't fit into the oven, so I had to separate the body for baking. Needless to say, one idea led to another, and since the head and the neck were cut apart, I cut the body into three pieces while it was baking, then glued everything back together on the painted board. While the pieces were cooling, there was a tremendous cracking sound, and the head split in two. After my tears of frustration dried, I glued the face back together consoling myself with the fact that painting was part of my plan. Paint covers the crack and the backing board gives enough support so that no more cracks have occurred.

Making a face out of flattened Baker's Clay dough is not as difficult as you may think it is.

Figure 131

69

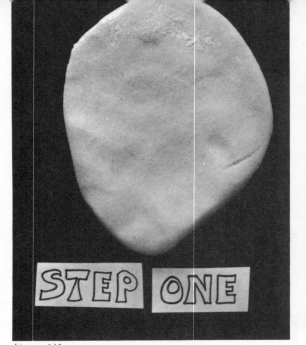

Figure 132

Figure 133

(FIGURE 132) *Step One:* Cut an oval from ½-inch flattened dough, place it on your cookie sheet.

(FIGURE 133) *Step Two:* Cut two dough ovals, position as eyes. Cut two more ovals, cut them in half, and position as eyelids.

(FIGURE 134) *Step Three:* Cut a dough triangle, position it as the nose.

(FIGURE 135) *Step Four:* Use your knife blade and flatten the edges around the eyes and nose. If the dough doesn't smush together easily, wet the entire surface. This moisture will bake away, and the wetness will enable you to smooth all cut edges together.

Figure 134

Figure 135

Figure 136

Figure 137

(FIGURE 136) *Step Five:* Cut a small mouth out of dough flattened to ⅛-inch thickness. Place the mouth in position, use your knife tip and poke the piece until you form skinny lips. Use your fingers to push the mouth into some sort of expression.

(FIGURE 137) *Step Six:* Use the knife tip to imprint smile lines or bags under the eyes. The more you embellish the basic face, the more interesting it will be when baked and basted and the less likely people are to notice that it may not be anatomically correct.

About Faces

Don't worry about making faces that are correct, beautiful or even humanlike. At first all my Baker's Clay faces turned out with noses and features resembling Charles de Gaulle more than anyone else, and although I struggled to create beauty, I always ended up with character. Even if you get lucky the first time around and make a face that is perfectly beautiful, chances are during baking some distortions will occur, so relax and accept that face as you've had to accept your own.

By now you should have gotten the message about accepting Baker's Clay for what it is, homey, organic, easy and *unreliable*. Hopefully you've made some pieces and now feel relaxed about the whole process of starting a project and following it through to completion. You've probably had some failures, and some disappointments

71

as well as some unexpected triumphs. Maybe what this book is really about is trying to learn to "hang loose" and accept Baker's Clay and life as it comes along, keeping an open mind and not expecting everything to be picture perfect all the time (or ever). You have probably also found out that often you start out with one specific project in mind, but will end up with something entirely different when you are finished. This change brings up an interesting and typical thing that often happens with creative handwork of all kinds. You start on a project with a definite finished piece in mind, but during the creating period, while you are actually working on the piece, your ideas change as new ones spring up. For example, last spring I was volunteered to make rabbit centerpieces (like the ones on page 49) for our PTA luncheon and somehow, most of the rabbits looked like fat and sassy Santas, so I turned them into Santas before popping them into the oven. The chairperson could not be swayed into changing the theme of the luncheon (Christmas in April?) so the Santas were packed away until Christmas, then I started again to make rabbits that looked like rabbits.

(FIGURE 138)   A Baker's Clay dollar bill, handsomely mounted inside a standard glass shadow box

Figure 138

(from the hobby shop) was made from dough flattened slightly thicker than cardboard. The pieces were cut out (very gingerly) with fingernail clippers and baked in a 200° oven for 2½ hours. The words "United States" are made out of alphabet soup noodles, pressed into the dough before baking. This project gives you the opportunity of making your own "bread" out of Baker's Clay.

72

(FIGURE 139) Houses or villas are fun to make and you can do as much embellishment as you want to in adding shingles, windows, porches, siding etc. Start by cutting the basic house shape out of ½-inch flattened dough. Place this shape on your cookie sheet. Flatten the remaining dough to ¼-inch (or even ⅛-inch) before you start to cut additional pieces. Be sure to moisten all overlapping or touching surfaces and bake this project at 250° for 3 to 6 hours, depending on the thickness of the layered areas. Baking at a lower temperature keeps the dough very light in color and usually doesn't

Figure 139

cause much distortion or swelling. Glue pieces of 4-by-4-inch redwood fencing blocks behind each piece to make it stand up. If you don't have a wide table or buffet to use to set houses upon, consider putting them in some sort of interesting shadow-box frame complete with trees etc.

73

So what have you learned?

Before you start on free-standing and assembled projects, review the processes and ideas covered in Flattening III—things like:

* You can make Baker's Clay projects that look more like fine art than something from the kitchen;
* Sources of design are everywhere. Try visiting the library, museum and local art shows to find ideas and inspiration;
* Baker's Clay and stained wood go together beautifully;
* You can bake pods and cones with the dough,—and get rid of pesky bugs at the same time;
* Cracks are to be tolerated or concealed with glue and paint;
* Projects which have to fit together are best done with the aid of patterns;
* Smush is a new term to use in describing Baker's Clay techniques—it combines smash and push;
* Dough can be colored with instant coffee before it is baked;
* Creativity, which you've always had and are always in the process of more actively developing, often takes amazing tangents—be tolerant and enjoy the trip!

7 FLATTENING IV— HARDEST BUT STILL NOT VERY COMPLICATED

Free-standing pieces are made out of ½-inch flattened dough, cut out in sections, baked, then assembled according to a plan. If you organize your thoughts and plans correctly, the finished project will stand up by itself. If you don't, and it doesn't, you can vacuum up the shattered pieces and start over again. The most important thing to keep in mind as you work is this. If the finished piece is to stand alone, it must be balanced.

In the beginning, I did a lot of vacuuming because the pieces just wouldn't balance. Often the solution to getting free-standing pieces to balance is to glue coathanger wire to the back side, then mount the piece on a wood block, a solution you'll want to remember in case your first projects don't stand too well either. Eventually, though, I figured out that necessary support had to come from large feet, three legs, or the proper stance so that the weight of the piece was in the middle, and then came up with the dough circles to place behind the supporting legs. It is easier to explain this technique by describing a project, so mix up some dough and make a free-standing piece, like Santa (FIGURE 141).

Figure 141

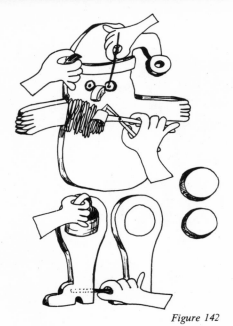

Figure 142

Figure 143

Figure 144

Flatten dough out to ½-inch. Draw the head and body on the dough, then cut it out. Draw two hip and leg pieces, keeping them identical. Place on the cookie sheet. Use your knife blade and try to make the feet bottoms as flat and even as possible. Insert small pieces of hairpins or paper-clip wire into the feet to give them added strength (see Fig. 142). Add embellishments like hair, face, beard and hands. Imprint designs and position arms over the beard (see Fig. 143). Prick all pieces with a sewing needle, then bake at 300° two or three hours. Remove from the oven and cool. Smear a layer of thick white glue over the back of all the pieces. Dry

Now assemble everything. Dab the glue on all touching parts, then place together. Carefully hold the figure upright to make sure that all supporting pieces are touching the table at the same time. Lay the piece back down on the table and support it with wads of foil or books or something to keep the legs and arms in proper position. Smear the glue really heavily over all the joints (on the back side particularly). After the glue dries, set the piece upright and let go, and if it stands up alone (see Fig. 143), congratulate yourself on being such a clever person. If the piece seems prone to topple over, your problem might be the fact that you didn't glue the legs on the body evenly. If this is the case, decide which leg is shorter, then dab glue on the bottom of that foot to make it longer—you may have to dab glue several times, drying in between dabs before you correct the imbalance.

Pieces that are nonhuman (by accident or design) are not nearly as difficult to make stand up, because their base of support is much better, i.e., four legs are better than two. A sitting creature provides a large base for support. For example, the reindeer (see Fig. 141) which is sitting down has the entire long leg piece for support. The back leg and hip are the same shape, and a circle of dough between the back hip and body are used to balance the piece.

Another way to make free-standing four-legged animals like the cow in Plate 15 is to use pieces shaped like this for support (see Fig. 144). After the pieces bake separately, glue everything together.

A third way to make pieces stand up is to bake support pieces, circles or platforms with the project. After baking, glue together, then paint. Check the illustration on page 68 ("Gingerclay House") to see how circles can be used to hold up flowers etc. You can also bake rectangular pieces to glue behind pieces to hold them up.

(FIGURE 145) "Napoleon Bonaparte" is but one of
the many figures from history you can make free-
standing. Others might be Caesar, Henry the VIII or
Noah.

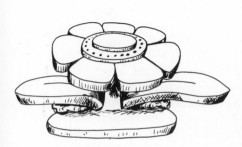

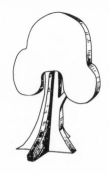

Proven favorites among the younger set are storybook characters, and the possibilities for ideas in this department are endless. Children's books are just crammed with adorable creatures that you can easily transform into Baker's Clay figures like Pooh and Eeyore (see Fig. 147). You can disregard the bit about making hip circles to go between legs and hip areas if you are making short, squat figures, because they won't be as tippy as taller ones. Pooh is supported by two legs, glued on after baking, and Eeyore's support comes from thick feet placed close together. In case you haven't guessed, the balloon over Pooh is not Baker's Clay, but is a large styrofoam ball, cut in half, then impaled onto the end of a piece of coat-hanger wire which was baked right in the figure

Figure 147

(FIGURE 148) Supports can be arranged in many different ways, as illustrated by this rocking horse. The legs were baked onto the rails, then glued to the body which had been baked separately. This piece was sealed, then painted with bright colors directly over the light, natural color of the dough. There are any number of creatures which you can make into rocking animals like lambs, unicorns, elephants, lions, cats, etc.

Designs for free-standing pieces can be as simple or as complicated as you want to make them. The three clowns, seen in color in Plate 14, are all one piece, and the most difficulty came in trying to draw the three characters together on the dough so all could be cut out at the same time from one slab. I had to make several clowns doing handstands before one would stand up

Figure 148

79

alone. The three-point approach used here, two hands and a hat brim, give adequate support, making this piece balance very well. When you are finished with projects as "tippy" as these, it is essential that you brush white glue on the back of the pieces.

It is the nature of things in our household for sculptures and other sitting-around-type *objets d'art* to be bumped by paper airplanes, footballs or clumsy kids, which is another reason why I always brush a layer of white glue on Baker's Clay things in the line of fire. White glue gives Baker's Clay, which normally has no child-resilient properties, a coat of plastic protection against unplanned knocks and flying objects. A coat of acrylic paint also increases the strength of Baker's Clay. The decision over what to paint and what not to paint (for protection) is certainly up to you. In making the decision you should probably take into consideration the number of small people in your household and the frequency things are upset, knocked over, tipped or bumped.

There are many brands of white glue on the market, found at the hardware, hobby or grocery store. Experiments with all types leads me to believe that your best for all around quality is Wilhold Glue, and one type in particular, heavy craft glue. It comes in a jar with a screw lid and is so thick that you can pick it up with your fingers, an advantage you'll understand as you are smearing glue on the back side of something. Glue this thick can be thinned with water to almost any consistency, so you can use it for other jobs around the house, and most important, when the glue is dry, it holds forever—despite rain, heat, or humidity. Buy the biggest container of glue you can find, because you'll use lots of it!

So what have you learned?

Flattening IV gave you some ideas on how to make Baker's Clay pieces stand up all by themselves and covered such important points as:

* Support arms or legs have to be spaced apart for proper balance, and this spacing is provided by small dough circles which you glue in place after baking;
* Small pieces of wire should be inserted into the dough in places where breakage might occur;
* White glue, smeared on the back sides of the pieces before assembling, will give a coat of plastic protection against unexpected tip-overs;
* Four-legged animals are easier to balance than the two-legged variety;
* Squat and lumpy figures do not require hip-circle support.

PINCHING AND WADDING I- EASY 8

About the Technique

Now you are ready to move on to a new technique, pinching and wadding, so named because that's how the dough is handled.

Fat and fully formed projects call for using rolled or wadded pieces of dough. Because the finished pieces are relatively thick, they require a much longer baking time than projects made from flattened and layered dough. Pinched and wadded projects tend to swell or flatten while in the oven, so it is best to prepare extra-stiff dough, as you did when working with the molds back in Flattening I.

Start by pinching off a piece of dough, then roll it into a ball between your palms. Decide what you're going to make, then pinch the dough ball or pat it out to form the bottom layer of the object. Add additional rolled lumps and bumps until you have finished the form. Your biggest problem will be making certain that the finished projects really are finished, because when the dough is extra-thick, like one or two inches, it might take as long as a full day to bake. You should turn the oven down to 250° to avoid having the piece turn dark brown, but if you plan on painting it, don't worry about the dark brown color.

It's not a good idea to take unbaked pieces out of the oven while you cook supper, then pop them back in afterwards. Reheating cooled pieces sometimes causes fractures and cracks. Plan ahead, work on the pieces early in the day so they can be baked before it's time to cook supper. Or, if you're not quite that organized, keep them in the refrigerator, covered with foil or plastic wrap until you can bake them uninterrupted. As a last resort, give the family peanut butter sandwiches or dine out. Occasionally I've had to bake food and Baker's Clay together and sometimes have found that dinner had a definite odor of flour and salt or that the project wafted a surrounding aura of dinner. You can speed up the baking process somewhat on these thick pieces if, after they have baked for several hours, you take them off the cookie sheet (using potholders, unless you have asbestos fingers) and place them directly on the oven rack. This allows the hot air to hit the piece from all sides, not just the top. But don't try speeding up baking flat projects, because flat dough curls like crazy if it is lifted off the cookie sheet before it is totally baked.

Small dough balls were rolled slightly flattened, imprinted, baked and basted, and seen on page 130 might be a good project for you to undertake to get the feel of this technique. One thing for certain, making decorated pebbles will give you the experience of watching some imprinted designs bake right out of the imprinted blobs if you didn't prepare the dough stiff enough to keep its shape while in the oven.

Figure 150

(FIGURE 150) Glue two paper-clip wire antennae to a Baker's Clay lump, then paint it to resemble a ladybug. Other materials on this plaque are a scrap of bark with moss conveniently attached, a scattering of straw flowers, a hunk of shingle and white glue.

83

(FIGURE 151) Macrame wall hangings often incorporate interesting beads, as do other types of woven, threaded or fabric wall pieces. If you are having difficulty locating some interesting beads, why not make your own out of Baker's Clay? The technique is similar to the one used for imprinting and baking the pebbles on page 130, except of course, you have to leave room in the bead center to string the cord through. You have several options in making the hole large enough so that the swelling, which always occurs during baking, doesn't close the hole completely. Use a plastic straw or unsharpened pencil to push into the dough ball before you print it on the sides. After you're done decorating it, push it off the pencil onto the cookie sheet (see Fig. 152). During baking, check occasionally to see that the hole isn't baking closed, and if it is, repoke with your pencil. Smaller beads don't need large holes, so just shape the bead, place it on the cookie sheet, then poke a small hole using a toothpick. All these beads were

Figure 151

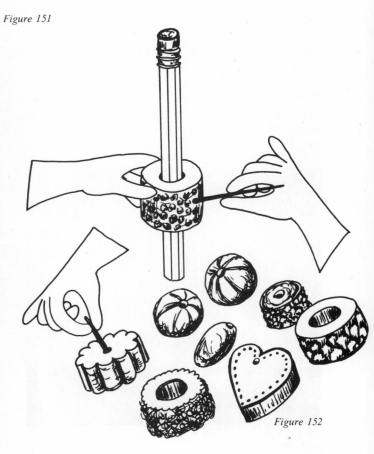

Figure 152

Figure 153

accidentally left in a 300° oven overnight (see Fig. 153). They not only look like wood, but feel like it too. Bake beads until you like the color, keeping in mind that you can always paint them if overbaking makes the color too dark to suit you.

(FIGURE 154) Here is another version of a Baker's Clay macramé holder. The shapes were patted into place, then imprinted around all edges with a toothpick. Bright green, red and orange paint make the holder look like a piece of glazed pottery.

Figure 154

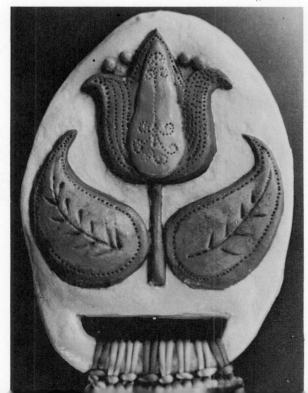

Figure 155

(FIGURE 155) As long as you are making beads, put some together with wooden beads to make an interesting necklace. These beads are decorated with small pieces of pinched dough used to form the flowers or designs, and were baked flat instead of standing on end. The pins a   ple pinched dough shapes, baked, painted, then glued to pin-backings from the hobby shop.

(FIGURE 156) Small wads of dough, shaped to more or less resemble snails, gain authenticity if you push real snail shells into the dough before baking. Wire antennae are hairpin pieces also pushed into the dough before baking. If your family isn't too keen on eating *escargots* (snails), you can find empty shells at the hobby shop, or might try to figure a way to exterminate the snails devouring your garden, and use their shells. As a last resort, form a Baker's Clay shell, then paint the stripes on it so it will resemble a real one.

Figure 156

Making Snakes

Any six-year-old will gladly show you how to make a snake out of Baker's Clay; after all, this process is only slightly removed from Mud Pies and is usually the first thing that any small child will do if handed a wad of prepared dough. If you can't locate a six-year-old child, try it on your own. (Fig. 157) Pinch off a piece of dough, roll it between your palms until it starts becoming elongated, or place the dough ball on your forth until the snake begins to appear (see Fig. 158). forth until the snake begins to appear (FIGURE 158).

(FIGURE 159) Young and old friends alike will love to receive their very own "creepie" to place under a floral arrangement, or just to leave sitting around someplace. The "creepie" has garlic-press hair and his stupid facial expression was made by cutting through the dough, opening the mouth, then letting it fall back closed (see Fig. 160). During baking slight swelling added to the loopy expression.

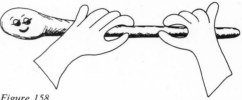

Figure 157

Figure 158

Figure 159

(FIGURE 161) Make a 3-foot-long snake, then wrap it around a straight-up-and-down glass jar (which has been wrapped with foil). Start wrapping at the bottom and work your way up until you either run out of dough or glass. Add a creepie head, bake four hours, cool, then slide off the glass. After painting, add a felt-covered

Figure 160

Figure 161

Figure 162

piece of cardboard to seal the bottom, fill with pencils, candies, nuts or lollipops, and present to the small child of your choice.

(FIGURE 162) Simple wood plaques like these are super-easy to make and are thoughtful gifts, particularly if you choose a word that has some particular meaning to the recipient. You can either bake the words directly on top of the wood, or bake them separately, then glue them on top of the prepared and stained wood.

(FIGURE 163) Lumpy candleholders are quick and easy to whip up and look unusual when grouped around a dining table centerpiece. Although the shapes may look to you like solid Baker's Clay, actually they have an inner core of aluminum foil, wadded tightly and surrounded by dough. The purpose of using foil inside really super-thick projects is twofold: first, it cuts the baking time in half, second, it gives the piece inner strength so it won't split or crack as much as if the piece were solid dough. Here's how to do it:

Figure 163

(FIGURE 164) *Step One:* Wad up some foil to form a ball the size of a walnut. Roll up a tennis ball-sized wad of dough.

(FIGURE 165) *Step Two:* Push the foil ball down into the dough. Find an empty bottle cap (the screw-on variety) and push this into the dough on top of the foil ball.

(FIGURE 166) *Step Three:* Apply cut strips of dough to embellish the outside of the wad. Bake 5 to 8 hours at 300°, or lower, if you wish the color to remain light. Cool, then paint and seal.

Angels

The ageless appeal of angels make them favorites for you and the family to make to deck your tree or put on packages or give to someone special.

(FIGURE 167) Angels don't have to be created just

Figure 167

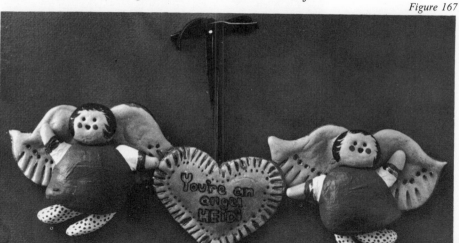

for the holidays—consider putting two together (with a hunk of wire in the dough between the figures) to make commemorative plaques to honor weddings, birthdays, anniversaries, graduations, new jobs, new homes, good deeds or nice people.

And who says angels have to be flatchested and without a certain amount of oomph? The beauty in **Plate 18** was created by a 35-year-old father who took a Baker's Clay class with his grammar school son during a PTA family crafts evening. While other crafters worked on more conventional angels, he made one designed to have special appeal to males.

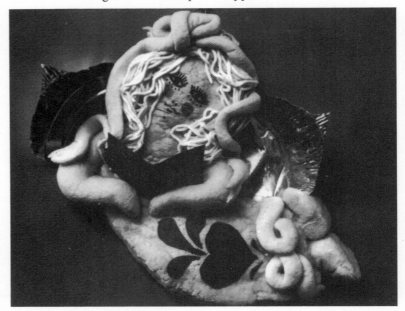

Figure 168

(FIGURE 168) Still another variation are Victorian-era angels, embellished with curlicues made from very small Baker's Clay snakes and with wings cut from pie tins of frozen meat pies. After the angel head and body are on the cookie sheet, push the cut pieces of pie tin into and under the dough. Sometimes Baker's Clay doesn't stick very well to foil, so you might have to secure the wings later with white glue.

And Now a Cherub

Start to roll some balls of dough to make a figure, in this case, a charming angel, cherub or winged person (see Fig. 169).

(FIGURE 170) *Step One:* Pat out balls of dough to form the wings, head, body, then roll dough to make two small, snakelike arms and legs.

(FIGURE 171) *Step Two:* Push and pinch the wings into shape, flute the edges with a fork or one side of the toothpick, then place them on a cookie sheet with the sides touching.

(FIGURE 172) *Step Three:* Place the dough snake in place to make the legs.

(FIGURE 173) *Step Four:* Push and pinch the largest remaining ball of dough to form the dress; place this over the legs. Pull up one side of the dress to give the figure the look of motion.

Figure 169

Figure 170

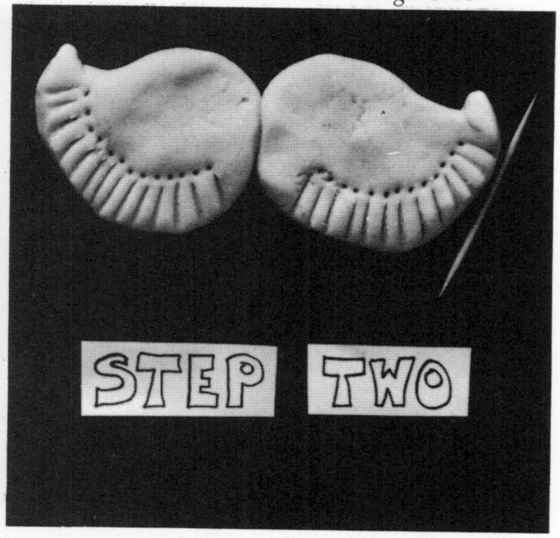

Figure 171

Figure 172

Figure 173

Figure 175

Figure 174

(FIGURE 174) *Step Five:* Cut the remaining dough snake in half and position the pieces as arms.

(FIGURE 175) *Step Six:* Roll the head ball between your palms until it is totally smooth; then position it at the dress top. Use a toothpick to poke eyes and mouth and push a hairpin into the top of the head to serve as a hanger.

Step Seven: Bake 4 to 6 hours at 300° or until done. Lift off the cookie sheet after two hours of baking and place the figure directly on your oven rack.

Step Eight: Cool, paint and seal. Hang up with bright ribbon or leather thong.

"Dough Dolls" in Plate 17 are one of several variations of lumpy figures you can make easily. Small, thick pieces like these, baked at a slow oven temperature of 200° will have to stay in the oven, uninterrupted for two or three days. Part of the charm of the figures is the fact that they are so light in color, yet trying to achieve this charm will most likely upset your cooking schedule. Speed up the baking time by using wads of aluminum foil or pieces of wood inside the figures.

Figure 176

Create Your Own "Dough Doll"

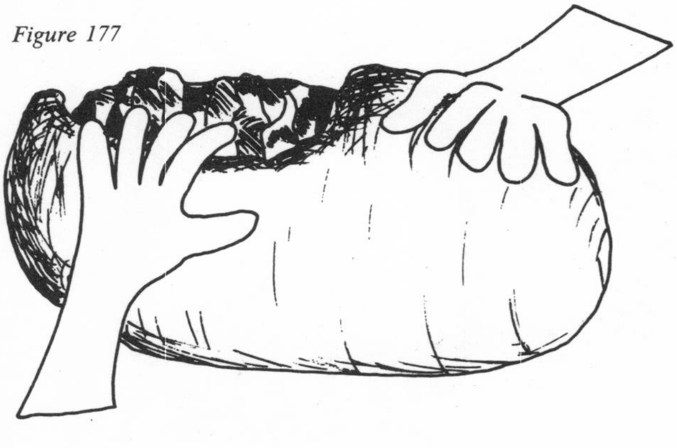

Step One: Wad up some aluminum foil to make a rectangular packet 1 inch wide by 2 inches long by ¾ inches thick (see Fig. 176). Pinch off some dough, roll it into a ball between your palms, slightly flatten it and place this over the foil, forming the doll's basic body (see fig. 177).

Figure 177

Step Two: Next roll a much smaller ball of dough and position this on top of one end of the dough-covered foil, making the doll's head (see Fig. 178).

Step Three: Now proceed in much the same manner as you did in making the angel. Pinch off dough, roll it into balls, then flatten to form the collar, apron, arms, hands, feet and hair. Imprint lines to make the hair, or use the garlic-press technique. As long as you are going to tie up the oven for a while, fill the cookie sheet with figures (see Fig. 179), varying clothes, but not poses. When the pieces are finished, cooled and sealed with a matte-finish spray, glue appropriate things into their hands. You can find small packages of assorted items like miniature rolling pins, baskets, stethoscopes etc. in the cake-decorating section or birthday party equipment section of your local supermart. Glue these itsy-bitsies between the hands of the figures. Miniatures are often made of plastic, therefore, shouldn't be baked with the dough dolls, unless you want the plastic to melt or burn and smell up the entire house.

"Fat Cats"

"Fat Cats" in Plate 19 started out to be quite small and full of detail. I did a lot of imprinting on the bodies after everything was put together, but the dough was much too soft and began to swell and enlarge almost from the moment I put them in the oven (which drives home my point about making the dough slightly stiff before making things using the Pinching and Wadding techniques!) I was really disappointed in the outcome and ready to throw the pieces away until my daughter interceded and suggested that I paint, antique and accent the pieces to show some of the detail which was lost during baking.

93

Figure 178

Figure 179

So what have you learned?

Now you have started to form dough freely by rolling and patting it into shapes of your choice, and you've learned that:

* Extra-thick projects require some planning so that the baking times don't interfere with trivia like cooking breakfast, lunch, or dinner;
* Pinched and wadded projects will swell despite all precautions, so don't bother pricking air holes.
* You should work with stiff dough when making projects using the techniques of Pinching and Wadding.
* Beads occasionally bake closed, so need checking while in the oven.
* Very fat projects will bake more quickly if you put a wad of foil inside;
* Projects which swell out of all proportion in the oven may be salvaged by means of clever painting techniques.

Gingerbread-like ornaments (5 inches tall and colored by the addition of instant coffee to the dough mixture) are easy to produce using paper patterns in the manner described on page 31.

Mushroom cluster (3 x 4½ inches) is a good project to "wet your feet" with when beginning to work with Baker's Clay. Other simple-to-make projects are seen on pages 21 through 28.

Plate 1

Plate 2

Plate 3

Plate 4

Above, *floral wreath (9 inches in diameter) is made of simple cut-out shapes. This project is also attractive left naturally colored and unpainted. Right, hanging basket (5½ by 7½ inches) has a pocket to hold letters. It hangs on a piece of leather thong. Look for easy-to-follow instructions on making hanging holders on page 51. Below, sun face (9 inches in diameter) was baked over an oven-proof bowl. The look of pottery was achieved by basting the piece with evaporated milk during baking as described on page 17.*

Plate 5

Plate 6

Plate 7

Top left, "*Knights and Castles*" (made with techniques described in Flattening II) is mounted inside an inexpensive 16-by-18-inch frame. The simple shapes were quick to cut out and gain added dimension by being glued onto a felt cut-out background. Top right, "*Baby Baubles*" (measuring 6 inches long) may be used to decorate for the holidays or to grace any blank wall space. Techniques for making them are in the beginning pages of Flattening II.

Right, "*Happiness Street*" (14 by 16 inches) illustrates a combination of several framing techniques. Bottom left, "*Victorian Villa*" (mounted on a piece of painted scrap lumber measuring 14-inches-square) illustrates all of the techniques described through Flattening II. This project retained a light natural color while baking and the Selective Surface painting technique was used to add color. Bottom Right, "*Christmas Is Coming*" (mounted inside a 24-inch-square frame) illustrates the use of simple imprinted shapes (ornaments) and an uncomplicated figure. The pieces were sprayed with matte varnish for a non-shiny finish.

Plate 8

Plate 9

Plate 10

Plate 11

Above left, "Christmas Colossus" (measuring 5½ by 3½ feet) is a super-sized project best undertaken by a group of bakers. The pieces were cut out using patterns and following a general plan. All pieces were antiqued with brown acrylic paint after painting, then sprayed several times with high gloss polyurethane varnish to make them resemble pottery. Above right, "Sir George" and "Clancy the Dragon" are layered pieces similar to those described in Flattening III. Scraps of material are used for the backing fabric placed inside cheapie metal frames.

Plate 14

Plate 13

Plate 12

Plate 15

Opposite page, bottom left, "Mother and Child" (framed in a heavy, rough shadow box measuring 13 by 17 inches) was constructed using methods described in Flattening III. Dark red acrylic paint antiqued with black gives a pottery look to the project. Opposite page, bottom right, Clowns (9 inches tall) are completely sealed with a coat of bright acrylic paints. They are balanced to stand alone using the method described in Flattening IV. Above right, "How Now Bread Cow" stands alone using another method of balancing as seen in figure 144 on page 76. Below, Hippo and Alligator (standing approximately 3½ inches tall) are projects which appeal particularly to children. Animals are easy to make following instructions found in Pinching and Wadding I.

Plate 16

Plate 17   *Plate 18*

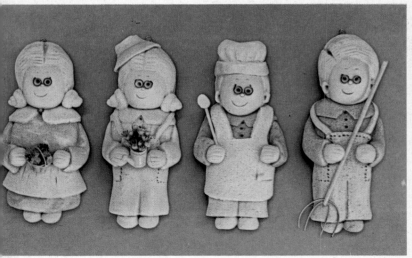

Above, *"Dough Dolls" (measuring 6 inches long) are colored by the addition of food coloring added to the dough mix during its preparation. Complete step-by-step directions for these little figures are found in Pinching and Wadding I.*

Above, *"Fertility Goddess" is painted with a mixture of food coloring and evaporated milk, using the Selective Surface method of painting. Instructions for making this paint are found in Chapter 10.*

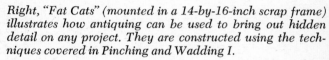

Right, *"Fat Cats" (mounted in a 14-by-16-inch scrap frame) illustrates how antiquing can be used to bring out hidden detail on any project. They are constructed using the techniques covered in Pinching and Wadding I.*

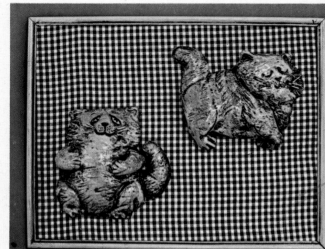

Plate 19

Plate 20

Above, "Cupid and Lady Love (8 inches tall) can be used to perk up plants or may be mounted on wood blocks. The pieces were basted frequently with evaporated milk during baking to turn them dark and leathery in appearance. Left, "Mon General" (11 inches tall) is painted by the Metallic Marvel method discussed on pages 117 and 118. Construction methods are similar to those discussed in Flattening IV and Pinching and Wadding II.

Plate 21

Plate 22

Plate 23

Left, "Madonna and Child" (11 inches tall) is made using simple pinched and wadded pieces of dough. This project sports the porcelain finish described on page 119. Above, "Hark the Ark" (24 by 19 inches) is an example of mounting Baker's Clay projects on quilted fabric.

9 PINCHING AND WADDING II— TAKES A LITTLE PRACTICE

Now that you have worked with flattened dough as well as with blobs and hunks of dough rolled into balls and snakelike shapes, try combining all the techniques in some projects we have labeled "zingers," handcrafted pieces which are sure to draw remarks like, "You're kidding, you baked that in the oven?" Some readers will probably never tackle a six-foot wall piece, a 400-pound camel or even a free-standing project, yet will enjoy working with flattened Baker's Clay dough ad infinitum. These involved projects are presented just in case you decide to be adventuresome or want to try your hand at something which you have never done before.

If you are one of those who insists on reading everything starting at the back pages—things like cookbooks, historical novels and whodunits, you may be rolling up your sleeves and getting ready to start on a project from this chapter. Don't do it! Start at the front of the book and make some projects using the techniques in the same order as presented. The zingers about to be described demand some mastery of Baker's Clay techniques. When learning to work with any new craft material, you don't logically start out on a project which requires some experience in dealing with the materials— to do that would be rather like deciding to learn to fly by soloing your first (and last) time in an airplane.

A new technique to use in pinching and wadding medium-sized forms is to add wire to the construction to give the piece enough strength so that it will stand up alone. As I mentioned before, anytime you bake Baker's Clay free-standing in your oven, you had better prepare yourself for the possibility of the dough slipping off the form and ending up in a pile on the cookie sheet.

95

Kneading additional flour into the dough will make it less likely to happen. If it does slip off anyway, be philosophical; scrape the blob off your cookie sheet and start over again.

The mushroom ring (see Fig. 181) gets its support from a frame of twisted florist's wire placed under the lumpy mushrooms as a base. After you twist the wire into form (see Fig. 182), pat and push the dough to cover the wire (see Fig. 183). Start working on this project directly on the cookie sheet, because until it is baked, the piece will be heavy, floppy and impossible to lift up all at the same time. Try to make the mushrooms so that they lean on each other for support. Or you might use some of your metallic cookie cutters, small glass jars or glasses to prop up a sagging mushroom until it has a chance to bake enough to stand up alone. If you can't find something to use for support, go back to that old standby, aluminum foil—wad a hunk of it up tightly, and use it as a supporting piece.

Figure 182

Figure 181

Figure 183

There are many things that you can stick inside Baker's Clay to give it strength and help hold it up during baking—the best are nails. These projects were made directly on top of pieces of interesting wood (see Fig. 184). The first time around, both projects puffed up while baking, then slid off onto the cookie sheet. Obviously, something had to be done to keep them on the

96

Figure 184

wood surface. The something in this case happened to be pounding in several large nails, almost as tall as the finished figure was to be. After the nails are in place, simply proceed as if you were patting dough around a wire frame, forming it into whatever as you work. If you look closely at the pieces, you'll notice that additional pieces of dough were used to hold the pinecones and pods. These flat pieces also have short nails placed under them to hold the dough in place while it bakes.

The "Lady on the Log" (Fig. 184) reminds me of a radical procedure which had to be done to salvage this particular project, a procedure which you'll probably need to know about sooner or later. In the first place, this project fell right off the log the first time it was popped into the oven. On the second attempt, much time and effort was spent sculpting a face that looked remarkably humanoid. Unfortunately though, as often happens, the face bubbled, puffed, sagged, ending up to look more like Grandma Frickett than some charming young thing sitting on a log contemplating her striped socks. Radical surgery appeared to be the only solution to salvaging the project, and the bread knife (or any knife with a serrated edge) turned out to be a most suitable tool to use. After the face was sawed away, a small dab of dough was placed over the surgical area, the piece was rebaked (lying flat so the added-on-piece wouldn't fall off), then painted. It is now much admired. Often you'll have projects with certain parts or rough edges that don't please you; so instead of chucking the pieces away in the trash can, get out the bread knife, and saw or cut off rough edges or other parts which

97

don't please you, then add new ones by rebaking with more dough or simply painting over the scarred area.

Take a few moments and study the faces of "Cupid and the Love Goddess" in Plate 20; then check the instructions in Flattening III on how to make a Baker's Clay face that is more or less humanoid. The only difference between these and the face of the "Bird Woman" on page 69 is that the first piece of dough, or head, was a slightly flattened ball of dough rather than a flat, oval piece. The remaining procedures to form nose, mouth, eyes and lids are exactly the same. Let me stress once again: fat projects will swell while baking, and often facial expressions and the faces themselves will change tremendously while in the oven. Since you can't control this, try to stay calm and enjoy the results, whatever they may be. Besides, you can always rationalize a super-ugly face as having tremendous amounts of character. No one will suspect!

Make—Ignore—Bake

Throughout this book the tendancy of Baker's Clay to swell while baking has been discussed, along with suggestions on how to cure lumps and bumps which you don't want or can't tolerate. While working on these projects, a new method of preventing swelling was discovered, and while it isn't the perfect cure-all for those bothersome lumps and bumps, it does prevent them 90 percent of the time. Experimentation with all sorts of projects using the flattening as well as pinching and wadding techniques have proven that if you air-dry Baker's Clay 7 to 11 hours, this prevents bubbling and also cuts down on the total baking time, since the projects dry partially before they go into the oven. The only problem is that occasionally fine cracks will form on the surface, though these are never major and don't continue to grow after the piece is baked. If you want to try this method of baking (and can plan your schedule around it), be sure to readjust the total baking time, which is usually cut in half, and check the pieces often so as not to overbake.

You may be grumbling that I should have told you about this method earlier in the book, and perhaps you're right. In my opinion, part of the job of working with Baker's Clay is that you can whip up lots of fun projects in an afternoon or evening and can finish them within a span of just a few hours. The Make—Ignore—Bake process requires a goodly amount of planning and rigid scheduling on your part. If you work on some projects during the day, you have to stay up with them at night while they bake. Conversely, if you make the projects at night, you'll have to drag your body out of bed at six o'clock in the morning to start baking. My personal feelings about schedules is negative. It's bad enough having to plan life around car pools, dentist appointments and automobile repairs; creative time should be fun and totally free from rigid schedules. So obviously, the only time I use this process is when I've spent many hours working on something full of intricate detail which is worth preserving (like the letters on the book cover).

And for you enthusiasts for itty-bitty projects, the "Madonna and Child" in Plate 22 should suit your needs for working on small projects. The figure is made of assorted pinched and wadded dough pieces, baked with wire inside, then painted and heavily glazed so it resembles porcelain. (This painting technique will be covered later.) The items I was referring to as itty-bitty are the small birds. You can, if you wish, try to hold tiny wads of dough and pinch them together to form a bird, or, pinch a piece of dough onto a toothpick, then add the other pieces working with eyebrow tweezers and a second toothpick. Personally, I'd rather repaint my entire house, alone, than attempt to make something as small as a $\frac{3}{4}$-inch bird. Small is definitely not my thing, but it may be yours. After the birds were formed, they were baked in a very slow oven 200° for one hour only, so they stayed light and didn't become too dry and brittle. To hold the birds upright in the oven, poke the other end of the toothpicks into the top of an egg carton to hold them up. Be sure that the egg carton is the paper variety, not molded plastic or styrofoam because there is no smell as horridly toxic as styrofoam slowly melting in the oven.

My children insisted that the lumpy beasties seen in Plate 16 be included in the book. They argued that Baker's Clay projects often end up in kiddie's rooms; so why not show mothers how to create creatures with particular appeal to children? So here they are. To make this type of free-standing project, put tightly wadded foil packets under portions of the project which you want raised slightly. To put it another way, the hippo is actually standing on his four fat little feet, with jaws dragging on the ground.

First wad a foil pad 1 by 4 by $\frac{1}{2}$ inches and place it on your cookie sheet. Next wad about $1\frac{1}{2}$ cups of dough

Figure 185

around a foil ball, then pinch and wad the dough to form a hippo head and body. Lay the body on the foil, making sure that the dough doesn't extend over the edge of the foil, and lay the head portion on the cookie sheet (see Fig. 185). Shape the legs, moisten, and press them into the body, then add eyes, hair and ears. Position the mouth by cutting it open as described in the "Creepie" project on page 87. After baking remove the foil, leaving a hippo standing on his four feet. You can use this technique of supporting lumpy animals with blocks of foil to create almost any type of creature which catches your fancy (or the fancy of your kidlets).

(FIGURE 186) "Love Lumps" are another type of project which use the principle of foil supports inside and out. The small arms holding signs were supported by foil wads during baking. Make the signs separately, then glue in place after painting. For some reason, lumpy forms, left smooth like these, often crack during or shortly after baking. Prepare to take your chances, and if you happen to know anybody who has recovered from a recent appendectomy or gallbaldderectomy, you can give them a Baker's Clay figure, with a small band-aid over the crack, carrying a sign "Congratulations on your recovery." If your friends are all healthy, fill the cracks with more dough, then rebake for 2 hours at 200°. You can make signs appropriate to cover most occasions from graduation to Valentine's Day.

I think you'll find it easy to handle these small lumpy shapes if you work continually on a piece of aluminum foil. This way you can turn the figure around by turning the foil, and can even pick it up to transfer to your cookie sheet handling the foil only. It's difficult to pick up a lumpy person without leaving your finger indentations all over it (or them).

Figure 186

Figure 187

(FIGURE 187) This "Happy Easter" centerpiece is a variation of the lumpy people. The rabbit ears originally stood up straight, but became bent and floppy during baking. Small pieces of wire in the ears would have given them enough inner strength to stand up—but as I've said before, the omission of wire was made. I've grown used to the cockeyed expression and loppy ears, and have learned to accept and enjoy them this way.

Before going on to another new technique or idea, don't forget that you can bake pinched and wadded projects over or around things just like you did in Flattening II. For example, this metallic-appearing mirror was baked over a foil-covered ovenproof soup bowl (see Fig. 188).

If you decide that you want to make some shaped pieces with open centers, try this technique. First cover the bowl (or whatever you are going to use to provide the shape) with aluminum foil, then place on the cookie sheet. Add leaves and fruit and vegetable shapes around the edge of the bowl, leaving an opening in the center. Bake, paint or seal, then glue a small mirror inside the opening. You'll have to do a little planning ahead to make sure that the opening you leave is the right size for the mirror you have selected. An easy way to do this is to trace around the mirror shape onto the foil-covered bowl, using a felt-tip marking pen. Then, as you shape the pieces around the border, you can make sure they extend slightly over the drawn line.

If you feel slightly overwhelmed trying to free-form

Figure 188

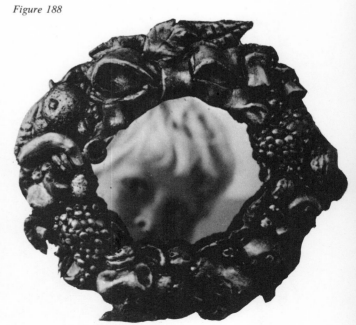

101

Figure 189

or create a pinched and wadded shape more complicated than an angel, here's a marvelous trick that will make the task less formidable. The carousel horse (see Fig. 189) utilized a technique borrowed from Flattening I. First flatten the dough to a thickness of $\frac{1}{4}$ inch. Either make a pattern from this picture and the technique discussed on page 31, or draw the horse shape directly on the dough, omitting the tail. Remove the horse shape to your cookie sheet and position it exactly as you wish the finished project to appear (see Fig. 190). Now, pick up a wad of dough, pinch off a little piece, roll it between your palms and position, for example on a front leg. Continue adding pinches and wads of dough until the horse is totally shaped (see Fig. 191), and don't be concerned about the fact that the flattened piece upon which you build the horse still shows. Nobody will notice it! Last of all, cut out flattened pieces of dough to make the bridle and saddle, use pinched and wadded pieces to make the flower and the striped post, and use your garlic press to form the abundant tail, mane and forelock. Be sure to place a wad of foil under the top of the saddle so you can later fill the pocket with lots of colorful straw flowers.

About those cracks: Off and on throughout this book I've talked about mistakes and problems like cracks. If you really eyeball this piece closely, you'll see cracks in the post, by the saddle, on one leg, and where the tail joins the body. These minor flaws, left and tolerated by our horse expert don't destroy the allover appearance of the finished project, in fact, will most probably never

Figure 190

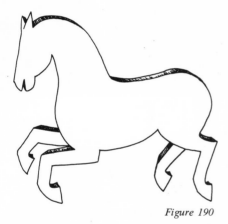

Figure 191

102

be noticed by admirers. All the cracks have been repaired, and none will cause disintegration of the horse itself. What's more, if you get a kick out of looking for flaws, errors and mistakes, eyeball all the projects in the book, chances are that you'll find cracks in at least half of them—cracks which have been either repaired, ignored or tolerated. The moral implication here is that you shouldn't become distressed over slight imperfections in an imperfect craft form.

"Hark the Ark" seen in Plate 23 is a second example of combining simple flattening with pinching and wadding. Just like the horse, the entire piece, animals, ark and all were outlined on flattened dough, then transferred to two cookie sheets. Additional pieces of dough were placed on top to form the animals.

After you gain some confidence working with pinched and wadded forms, and can combine pieces of dough with ease, you might want to tackle a project like "Adam's Apples" (see Fig. 192). All pieces were baked at a very low oven temperature so there would be no browning, and the figures were left that light color. Working on a project that has several separate pieces can present a problem in trying to keep everything the proper size. Since conventional patterns can't be used with pinching and wadding, you might want to try another method. First draw the pieces to size on paper, then cut them out and trace around them using a felt-tip marking pen and drawing on to aluminum foil. Then pinch and wad away, filling in the outline to form the figures, leaving them on the foil to bake.

(FIGURE 193) You don't have to live in New York to create pop art. Some of you might not be too keen about having an inedible hamburger sitting around as an art object, but at least it is fun and nonfattening. Concoct any type of food like a hot dog, bacon and eggs, a peanut butter sandwich or a supersized Oreo cookie. Come to think of it, with inflation and food prices what

Figure 192

Figure 193

Figure 194

they are, creating the common hamburger might be more of a memorial than anything else. The hamburger was constructed in layers, just like the real thing: a bottom bun, meat imprinted with the end of a straw to make it resemble ground beef, a square of cheese, lettuce and the onion rings. At this point I realized that the thing was 3 inches thick and would have to cook for days, so I cut out the center with a circular cookie cutter, inserted foil to fill the hole, added the top bun piece and baked away. Basting during the last hour of cooking turned the bun to a realistic brown.

Pinched and wadded projects don't always have to be large or bulky. You can work with very small bits of dough to form little things like the flute, fingers, cheeks and eyes on the marchers in this project (see Fig. 194). Build and layer similar figures like you did your first angel. Start by making the bottom layer first, which in this case is the basic body, legs and heads. Then add arms, hands, instruments, hair, hats, and last, clothing tabs and buttons. The flautist stands out from the others because he has been glued on two empty thread spools, one behind his head, the other behind his back leg

And last, but not least, one of my favorites, "Granny Goodtime" (see Fig. 195), a charming little ole lady who knits sweaters for snakes. A long time ago, back in the dark ages when we were children, a favorite bedtime story book was full of the adventures of this marvelous Granny, complete with high-top boots and always armed with two trusty knitting needles (more effective weapons than those arm bands on Wonder Woman).

Figure 195

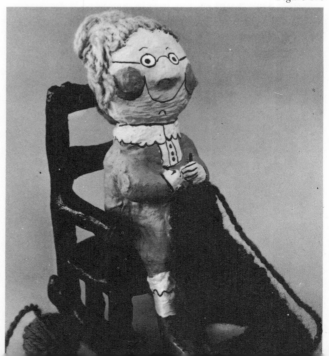

Anyhow, during out last move, we found and opened a box of old books, and there she was, still with as much appeal as when I was a child. After much consideration about how to make Granny shapes like the Granny in the book (memories must be true to form you know!), I decided to make her in sections (see Fig. 196). After baking, painting and assembling, something was very wrong. Granny didn't look good with a flat head (from the portion of the head lump which had baked flat on the cookie sheet.) A small wad of foil gave the back of her head some shape, and a coat of glue and lavender yarn covered the foil. Granny came into Baker's Clay being on an evening when Dear Him was out of town on business. Long about midnight, I discovered that our two knitting needles, needed to make the snake scarf couldn't be located. Talk about being on the horns of a dilemma, I mean, do you have a neighbor who would loan you knitting needles at midnight? The solution, as usual, turned up in the garage tool kit. Did you know that it is possible to knit with two nails, and that you can whip out a piece of flawed material 10 by 1½ inches in only two hours—if you stick to your task without letting things like dropped stitches, cramps in your fingers or that TV test pattern that comes on at one o'clock deter you. This project has to be the best definition of that expression, an exercise in insanity.

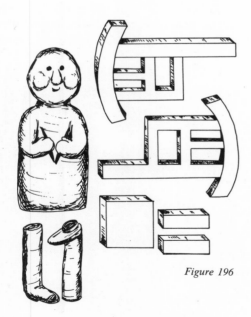

Figure 196

105

So what have you learned?

* Wire placed inside pinched and wadded figures gives them needed support.
* When working with Baker's Clay on top of a hunk of wood, pound some nails partially into the wood, then build the shape on top of the nails.
* Mistakes which occur during baking can usually be surgically remedied.
* The Make—Ignore—Bake method usually prevents swelling and distortions from occurring during baking.
* Four-legged creatures are easy to bake on top of foil supports.
* You can combine flattening techniques with pinching and wadding while working on an involved project.
* You can use patterns with pinched and wadded projects.

10 FINISHING TECHNIQUES AND FRAME JOBS

It's not what you've made, but what you do with it that counts!

During early experimentation with Baker's Clay I discovered that painting and framing could make a simple project look like a fantastic work of art. On the other hand, a sloppy job in the finishing and framing department will make the project look crummy. Many finishing and framing techniques have been used to show you how many different ways there are to complete Baker's Clay projects. Some of these techniques are simple, some involved, none very difficult to master.

At first you will most likely be content with making simple, cut-out shapes that hang directly on the wall. Eventually though, you will want to do something special with a piece you've just completed, and you'll need the information offered in this chapter. For simplicity's sake, painting and finishing have been separated from framing and mounting, because you obviously have to paint the piece before you stick it in a frame or on a board.

Finishing Techniques

There's more than one way to add color to Baker's Clay. The first and most simple method of coloring Baker's Clay is to do absolutely nothing with it, letting the natural color of the dough brown and develop as it cooks.

Basting

To make the dough a dark, rich brown, baste with evaporated canned milk during the last one hour or half hour minutes of baking. In order to produce very dark brown pieces of Baker's Clay, baste continually during their entire baking time, like the figures in Plate 20.

Other kitchen materials which you can use to baste Baker's Clay include egg yolk, mayonnaise, a mixture of sugar and water, and egg white. Some afternoon when you have nothing better to do, whip up some pieces, then baste each one differently, using these assorted foods to see exactly how each colors the dough. These alternatives to milk are mentioned here because they do change the dough color and are readily available.

Internal Coloring

"Gingerclay House" on the cover illustrates the method of tinting Baker's Clay internally, adding color to the dough before it is baked. Instant coffee is excellent to use and you may use as much or as little as you like to change the color to various shades of brown. For some reason, mixing instant coffee into the water you are using to prepare the dough also changes the consistency of it slightly. You'll need to add a little more flour and as the dough bakes, it will appear to have a slight sheen that uncoffeed dough doesn't have. Also, the dough will smell heavenly (assuming you like the aroma of fresh coffee).

You can achieve all sorts of pleasing pastel colors by mixing food coloring into the dough, adding as much or as little to reach the color you want the finished project to be.

The basic sun face, eyes, nose, and eyebrows (see Fig. 198) were cut from noncolored dough. Remaining rays and features were cut from dough tinted a dark pink. The hanger, a soda can pull-tab, was embedded in the dough before baking.

The Dough Dolls in Plate 17 illustrate a variety of food-color shades, ranging from light green to yellow to salmon pink. Mix the food coloring into the water before you add it to the flour, then mix and knead it together to reach a uniform color. However, if you prefer the color to be marbleized, prepare the dough, then sprinkle some food coloring over it and knead until the streaks and color variances please you. You might be thinking that if food coloring can be mixed into the dough, and is so inexpensive and easy to use, why didn't I tell you about this sooner? Well, there is this tiny little

Figure 198

problem involved with food coloring that keeps it from being the best way to add color to Baker's Clay. The color bakes right out of the dough; bakes absolutely away, leaving the dough almost the same color as if you had added nothing to it, UNLESS you bake the pieces at 200°. Low heat does not affect food coloring, not in the least, but it does affect your cooking schedule, because projects like the dough dolls take up to three days to bake at that low temperature. One other slight problem you'll run into using food coloring is that it not only colors dough, but also your skin and fingernails. Ordinarily, I don't mind having orange fingers. The color wears off in a day or so, but if you have to attend a bridge luncheon or appear in public, you'll get mighty tired of explaining your colorful hands. If you dissolve the food coloring in water, then add the salt and add it to the flour, mixing as long as possible with a kitchen spoon. You won't be in contact with it for long and won't have to be as concerned about its coloring your skin.

External Color—Paint

There are dozens of ways to paint Baker's Clay, and as many different materials on the market which you can buy to use. After experimenting with most of the products available, I think acrylic paints are your best bet to use on Baker's Clay. Poster paints have long been

109

a favorite among craftspeople, probably because these paints are inexpensive and can be found everywhere from hobby shops to grocery stores. Unfortunately, though, poster paint is generally unreliable when used on Baker's Clay. For some reason, it almost always chips and falls off, even though the piece is undercoated and sealed with a coat of spray paint.

Acrylic paints are the type used on most of the projects in this book (except the metallic-appearing ones) because they are easy to work with, give the kind of results you want, are nontoxic and reasonably inexpensive to buy. They come in either tubes or jars, have a latex base similar to house paints, don't smell, and are readily available in craft or hobby stores, hardware stores, large grocery stores and through various mail-order catalogs. You can thin acrylic paints with water if you want to; painted projects will dry in under 20 minutes. I use acrylics in tubes, mainly because they don't dry out as fast as acrylics in jars. To be totally honest with you, paint in jars doesn't dry out at all, unless you have my particular problem, which is an inability or unwillingness to screw jar lids down tight.

Acrylics are easy to work with, but do have a characteristic in common with most other types of paints: they are slightly transparent, and if you want to get bright or true colors, you'll have to undercoat the areas you plan on painting, using a product called gesso which is a highly refined flat white latex paint that covers any and all colors. All you need to do is to apply a coat of gesso on whatever you are going to paint, and when it dries, 20 minutes later, you'll have a nonshiny white surface to paint upon. Gesso is very much like acrylic paints, comes in several different sized containers, can be found wherever acrylics are sold, doesn't smell, is nontoxic and can be washed out of paintbrushes with soapy water.

Another plus for this product is that it gives a coat of latex protection to whatever project you happen to be painting, which might be very important if you are doing some plant perk-ups or free-standing pieces which stand the chance of being bumped, watered or otherwise manhandled. Projects which need only a simple outlining job or just dabs of paint don't need to be undercoated with gesso—use it when you are painting areas more than 1 inch wide.

You should buy or scrounge up about three good-quality paint brushes, one number 000 (that's a brush size) camel's hair for detail work, this brush is very small, has about 23 hairs in it and is good to use for outlining, and two slightly larger brushes to use when painting large areas. A good quality ½-inch-wide soft brush also comes in handy for basting your projects with milk while they are baking.

Some Baker's Clay buffs insist that only tempera or watercolors should be used on the pieces to preserve that natural look, and they may be right. Artist's watercolors, which come in tubes, are rather expensive, and don't cover as well as acrylics. In fact, you often have to paint something two or three times to cover the dough color completely, as watercolors are very transparent. As an alternative to using shiny acrylic paints, consider mixing up your own colors, using kitchen materials, which was done to make paint for the "Fertility Goddess" in Plate 18. Make nifty paints by mixing just a few drops of food color with a tablespoon of canned evaporated milk. You can mix any color you want except white.

Here's How to Do It

Prepare the colors so they are ready to paint on the project just before it is done cooking. Find a white plastic egg carton, and measure 1 tablespoon of milk into each compartment (first take out the eggs please). Shake a few drops of the desired color into the milk, mix it with a small spoon or your finger, keep adding more color, or other colors to make in between shades, until you have the hue you want. Mix up all the colors at one time, then prepare to paint the projects. Remove the pieces from the oven, paint, then rebake for eleven minutes to dry the milk. You'll notice that the painted areas have a slight gloss, and that the colors look slightly darker than if you had painted them with acrylics. After the pieces cool, spray them with sealer and then you're done. This method of painting is easy on your budget and ideal if you are working with a group of children. The only problem you're likely to encounter here is handling hot Baker's Clay projects for painting, then rebaking. If it is impossible to do everything at the same time, bake the pieces one day, allow them to cool, then paint and rebake on another day.

So Much for the Materials—March on to the Methods of Painting

Remember when you first learned to ride a bicycle. Naturally, you didn't solo around the block your first time out. You probably wobbled two or three feet, then fell off. Learning to paint Baker's Clay is much like learning to ride that bike, with many of the hazards removed—you can hardly expect to fracture a metatarsal if you make a mistake! Go back and study some of the simple-to-make projects in Flattening I or II. You'll see that many of them like the townhouse planter on page 29 are basted and have no paint on them at all. Others, like "Victorian Villa" in Plate 9 and the mushroom described in great detail on pages 19 through 21 are painted with a technique we call "dabbler's delight." Use burnt sienna (brown) acrylic paint, a small paintbrush and lightly dab or paint onto the outside edges only, leaving the rest alone (see Fig. 199). Dabbling or outlining doesn't add much color to the piece, but it does serve to accent the shapes and other details which you imprinted onto the dough before baking. So at first try to restrict your painting efforts to dabbling only.

When you first start to add some color to your Baker's Clay projects, you just might unleash a latent tendency towards Van Gogh's Syndrome. This is characterized by an overwhelming desire to put color on every visible and nonliving surface. If you are seized by the syndrome, go absolutely bananas and paint the project

Figure 199

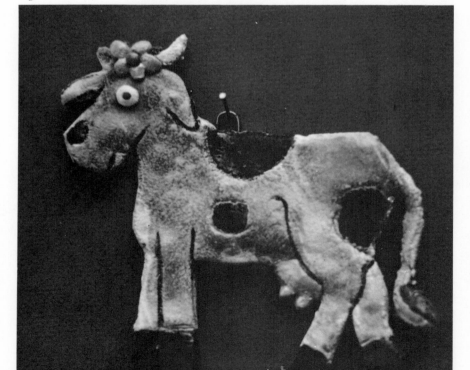

every color in the book (inventing several new hues along the way), and then decide you hate the outcome. Don't feel frustrated. You can salvage an overpainted disaster by turning it into a metallic marvel which will forever conceal your lack of painting control.

After you master the technique of Dabbling, go on to slightly more advanced "surface painting." Browse through the book again to find some projects which are painted sparingly, with color only on the tops (never extending down the aisles). The "Birds and Lollipops" (see Fig. 200) were designed to decorate a barren garden area during an outdoor luncheon. After lunch they were raffled off and went their separate ways to bring cheer and color to inside potted plants. All the pieces in the "Christmas Colossus" in Plate 11 are only partially painted, and only on top surfaces. Selective surface painting (not to be confused with the military process bearing a similar title) also requires some self-control—you have to stop at the edge, and if you are sloppy with your paintbrush, this can present a problem, though not an insurmountable one. You can always mix up some paint to match the dough, then paint over any mistakes which dribble down the sides. Begin by painting gesso over all areas which you plan to paint. Let the gesso dry for 20 minutes, then paint with acrylic colors. White plastic egg cartons make marvelous paint containers. Squeeze a little acrylic paint into one of the

Figure 200

compartments and thin the paint slightly with water, then brush away. When you're done painting, throw the carton away, or assemble several dozen paint-smeared cartons, hang all on the wall and call them impressionistic art.

And finally, after you become familiar with mixing colors and painting them on Baker's Clay surfaces, try painting all surfaces and sides—the *Whole Thing*. You should undercoat with gesso so your colors turn out bright, unless, of course, you want them to be dull and dark. If mixing and selecting colors which go together is hard for you, invest in a simple color wheel from the hobby or art-supply store. This will explain how certain colors work, or look, when placed side by side. It will also suggest or explain how to mix colors to reach certain in-between shades. At first you will probably become an expert at mixing two shades, gray and mud brown, which are the results of almost all mixing errors, but after a little while you should be able to blend the colors you want. It is not necessary to go into a lengthy discussion about color usage; all you have to do to get ideas is to look around you and pay particular attention to the color pictures in this book. Use these pictures as guides for selecting your own colors or color combinations.

When All Else Falls: Try Antiquing

Working with colors can be tricky at first, and sometimes you will not be pleased with the results: Certain colors which looked great on the color chart, simply didn't "work" or look good next to others. Quite by accident, I discovered the cure-all for disastrous color combinations, and that cure-all is known as antiquing. You have probably heard this term before. It's been around for a long time and is usually found in descriptions of painting techniques applied to refinishing furniture. Antiquing means "instant age" in arty circles, because the addition of brown or black in the cracks or crevices of anything, like a sculpture or chest of drawers, makes it appear to be instantly older than it really is. In crafting circles, Baker's Clay circles in particular, antiquing often means covering up a multitude of mistakes, like an inept painting job, improperly prepared dough, or after-baking cracks. "Mother and Child" in Plate 13 illustrates this point. Originally the piece was left natural, but it cracked down the front, so was repainted dark red, then antiqued with black paint. "Fat

Cats" in Plate 19 was a disaster from the very beginning. First the cats puffed out grotesquely while baking, and after painting they still didn't look like anything worth saving. Bright yellow, antiqued with black salvaged them. Antiquing brings out hidden detail, cracks and imprinting which may have turned dark during the baking process. The piece made in a mold on page 33 shows how much detail can be picked up by applying dark color in the most receding areas—another example of the advantages of antiquing.

The Process Is Simple to Master. There Are Two Ways to Do It.

Number one: Antique over the unpleasing colors with dark brown acrylic paint slightly thinned with water, dry, then seal with varnish.

Number two: Change the colors by painting the entire thing with gesso, repainting it one color only, then antiquing with either black or brown acrylic paints. Dry. Finish with a coat of varnish.

How to Antique

First of all, let's assume that you have made up your mind to antique over a color (and if you don't like the outcome, you can always regesso and start over again.)

(FIGURE 201) *Step One:* Set the object to be painted on lots of newspapers. Make sure that the surface is thoroughly dry before you start painting over it.

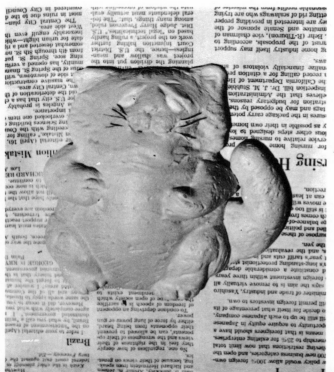

Figure 201

(FIGURE 202) *Step Two:* Mix black or brown acrylic paints with water using a 3 to 1 ratio—that's 3 parts of water to 1 part of acrylic paint. Use a ½-inch wide paintbrush to paint the piece completely with the antiquing mixture, making sure that you brush it into all the cracks and crevices and that not one bit of the under color is left showing through the paint.

Figure 202

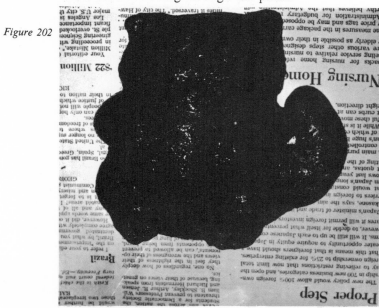

(FIGURE 203) *Step Three:* Quickly begin to wipe the black paint off all top surfaces, using paper toweling or an old soft rag. Immediately you'll see detail emerge as you wipe the paint off the top surfaces. Don't get overenthusiastic and wipe the paint off everything. The point is to leave it in the cracks and crevices and to wipe it off the top surfaces, (surfaces closest to you).

Figure 203

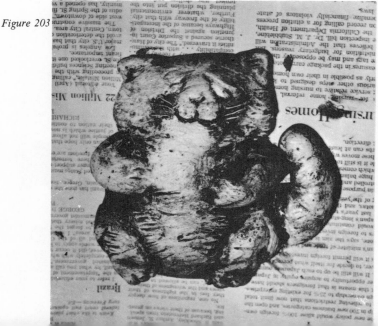

If, due to eager-beaverness you end up wiping off all the antiquing color, let the piece dry while you mix up more antiquing stuff, then begin again. As a last resort, if you botch it up or wipe so hard you remove the undercolor, you can repaint with the basic color and begin again. As soon as the antiquing dries, you'll see that the project looks absolutely scruddy (scroungy and dirty), which is just how it is supposed to look. Dry for 24 hours, then spray with varnish or resin to seal, and almost, magically, the moment the spray hits that scruddy-looking surface it comes alive with vibrancy and spirit (and so do you if you've been doubtful about the ultimate color resurrection).

Metallic Marvels

Earlier I mentioned how you can spray-paint disasters with metallic colors when all else fails. The process is one which you'll want to use on projects you want to look like metal (see Fig. 204) and not necessarily just on those which you want to disguise. You'll need to invest in some spray paints, which if cared for properly, should give you more than enough paint to cover dozens of metallic marvel projects. Buy a can of flat black enamel, brown enamel and a can of metallic colored enamel, either gold, brass or copper. I use copper spray because it is dark to begin with and makes the finished color look more authentically metallic. You'll also need to buy either a tube or small jar of light gold or silver metallic coloring wax. This product is found at the hobby shop or hardware store and you apply it with your finger to highlight desired surfaces.

Figure 204

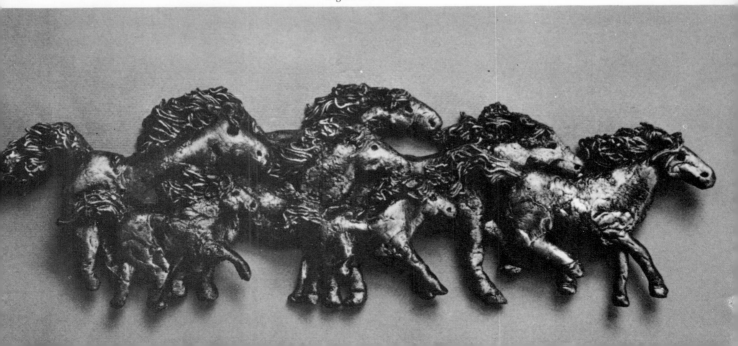

Go outside and spread newspapers all over the ground, then place the gessoed piece in the center of the newspapers. Shake the three cans of color so they are ready to be used and start by spraying the piece with flat black. Do not allow this coat to dry, but immediately spray brown heavily into all cracks, directly over the black. At this point, the two colors should be floating on the surfaces of the piece. Respray with black again, trying to concentrate more or less on the higher and smoother areas. Now stand back, hold the copper spray can four feet above the piece and quickly push the nozzle three or four times, releasing small clouds of copper film which drift over and land in spots on top of the wet-painted surface. This very light coat of metallic color is the one that gives that look of poured metal. If too much metallic spray gets on the piece, start the process all over again with a coat of black paint. When the colors please you, stop spraying and let everything dry for at least 24 hours (inside the garage, please, not outside in the moist night air).

Now for the final dramatic touch: At this point, your metallic project should look pretty good to you, but there is one more step that will give it that special look, that zing and oomph which will cause people to remark that it can't be Baker's Clay! Rub your forefinger into some of the coloring wax, then carefully start to rub the wax onto the top surface closest to you, giving these surfaces highlights and accentuating the darkness of the still-darker cracks and crevices. I guarantee that it won't take you long to master just the right touch with this highlighting business, and the results will be well worth your efforts. Keep in mind that you are highlighting only, not giving a whole new color to the piece. Look for rough surfaces or embellishments like buttons, features, hair, arms, fingers, etc. to highlight. Don't fool around with flat uninteresting surfaces. If you highlight too much, and the piece looks like it has the Midas touch, take it outside, spray with black, then repeat the painting process. Be sure to spray the back side if the finished piece is to be free-standing or sticking out of a plant. In fact, use the back side as a good place to practice highlighting. A final coat of clear varnish is not necessary as you have totally encapsulated the piece with enamel paint and shouldn't ever have to worry about moisture seeping in. If you want to add a slight bit of color under the metallic highlights, as I did in "Mon Général" in Plate 21, do so by painting with acrylic paints after you have finished spray painting and before you highlight with coloring wax.

The Porcelain Finish

It's not really very difficult to make Baker's Clay look like glass like "Madonna" in Plate 22. However, there are a few basic steps which you must take during the creation of the piece to insure that you have a smooth and light surface to paint using this process.

First of all, lumpy dough cannot be painted to look like glass, so be sure to knead the dough for the full ten minutes so it is smooth and grain-free.

Second, as you place the pieces onto your cookie sheet, be sure to use your wet finger or a table knife to smooth those rough edges totally away.

Third, bake at 200°, no higher, so the dough will not swell or bubble and will not brown or turn any color at all. Bake the piece at least two times as long as you would at 300° to make sure that it is completely baked. Cool, then start on the process.

First paint features, or add color wherever you want it. Keep in mind that porcelain is rarely dark or somber in color, so use bright and vibrant shades. Dry. Let the paint dry, then brush a layer of glue over all. White glue gives depth to any painted surface, making it look like glass. So, start by brushing a layer of white glue over the entire piece. If you have the thick type of glue, thin it slightly with water so you can brush it on easily. Brush slowly and carefully to avoid making bubbles. (They dry as bubbles!) Let the surface dry for 30 minutes. When the glue is wet it will appear to be cloudy. This will turn to a clear glaze when it dries. Give the entire piece at least three more coats of glue, allowing it to dry at least one hour in between coats. Finish with a spray coat of high gloss varnish or resin.

Frame Jobs

Now that you know how to paint, stain, antique or spray your Baker's Clay creations, it's time to look at some devastatingly simple ideas for framing. Don't feel overwhelmed at the suggestion that you should make frames and do other complicated appearing things to make your Baker's Clay look attractive and professional. In the first place, you probably will never have to make a frame. If you know a person who is handy with a hammer and saw, perhaps you can con them into making some simple frames for you. If you don't know a

119

woodworking enthusiast, or aren't good at conning, buy picture frames in the dime store, hobby shop, hardware store, art supply store or through the mail-order catalogs. Being a natural scrounger, I adore going to rummage, white elephant, garage or patio sales, and find most of my frames in these places. The possibility also exists that with all the attractive alternatives, you may never put a frame around any piece of Baker's Clay you've made.

Alternatives to Framing

One: If the project is reasonably small and light in weight, push a hairpin into the top to serve as a hanger-upper. This type of hanger was used extensively on projects found in Flattening I.

Two: Projects which seem to be too heavy to be held up by thin hairpins might be candidates for pull-tabs from soda cans. (Fig. 205) After you finish forming the project, carefully lift up the top and push the tab portion down into the dough. Keep pushing until the whole thing is embedded and the top of the ring is all that shows. If you forget to bake a hanger into a piece which you want to hang directly on the wall, you can glue it on afterwards when the project is finished.

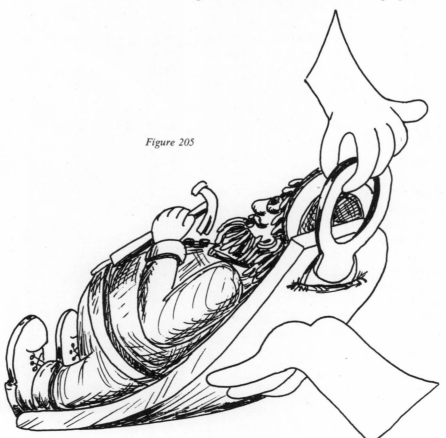

Figure 205

Figure 206

Figure 207

First glop some thick craft glue on the spot where you want the hanger to go, then push the tab and ring into the glue (see Fig. 206), leaving just enough ring left out to slip over a nail on the wall. If you used enough glue, it should take several days to dry. If you didn't, the piece will do a Humpty Dumpty off the wall when it pulls away from the hanger.

Three: (Fig. 207) If you poke holes in the project before you bake it, then all you have to do to hang it up is to find some leather thong, yarn or brightly colored heavy string, thread this through the holes, tie a bow and you're done.

Four: Projects baked with pieces of coat-hanger wire in them are ready to go as soon as they have been painted . . . simply find a dull plant that needs perking and push the wire down into the soil. If you don't intend the projects to function as plant perk-ups, but rather to stand alone in a block of wood, then you need to know how to drill a hole in wood if you don't have a drill. This can present a formidable obstacle if you don't have a hand or electric drill, friendly neighborhood woodpecker or obliging person to drill a hole for you. There is a very simple method of poking holes into objects you are going to use for mounting Baker's Clay pieces, and the procedure doesn't require extensive equipment.

121

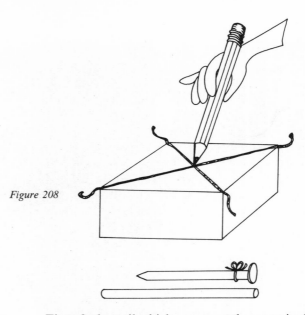

Figure 208

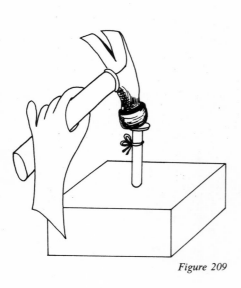

Figure 209

First, find a nail which measures the same in diameter as the coat-hanger wire (see Fig. 208). Ask at the hardware store if you can't find one in the toolbox at home. In our household, this nail is known as the BAKER'S CLAY NAIL, and is tied with a piece of bright red yarn to hang on a hook in the garage . . . which saves me from hours of searching to locate the darn thing everytime I need it. The red yarn identifies the nail as something special, not to be used for building a fort, a go-cart or something frivolous. Besides the nail, you'll need two pieces of string, a hammer, pencil, and of course, the scrap wood block. Position the block as it will ultimately stand with the Baker's Clay piece on it, lay the strings corner to corner, and make a pencil mark where the strings cross. This should be the exact center of the block and the mark is the place where you'll hammer in the nail. Hammer the nail into the wood to a depth of 1 inch (see Fig. 209), then carefully remove the nail (and don't bend it in the process or you'll need to find another nail for the next project). Hang the nail back up where you found it, and admire your handiwork . . . for the hole which the nail made is sitting ready and waiting to receive the coat-hanger wire which is sticking out of your Baker's Clay piece. If you are going to use the wood block for a candleholder, like the project on page **64,** after you pull the nail out, find another one the same size, and pound it, head down, into the block, leaving the pointy end sticking up. Cover this end with a piece of foil or masking tape, and finish the project. When it's done, remove the protection and push your candle down over the nail to hold it securely in place.

About Bases

Regular wood is preferable over balsa wood or styrofoam because Baker's Clay, as you may already have discovered, can be very heavy, and if the supporting piece is not sturdy, the finished project will be topheavy, and topple over because of this.

You should never have to buy wood to use as a mounting base . . . not ever. In fact, the only time I *buy* wood is when simple forms and straight pieces are needed to make frames. Scrap lumber can be found anywhere buildings or homes are under construction. Locate the scrap pile which is usually located behind the building or home, then find the construction foreman and ask if you can help yourself to some wood scraps. If you're lucky, he won't ask why you want it, because this usually results in a lengthy discussion of your Baker's Clay interests and his telling you extensively about his cousin in Fresno who crochets baskets out of eucalyptus pods. If you are questioned about why you want the wood, consider taking "creative license" and telling a fiblet about your cub scout troop needing wood scraps to make bird feeders. Take as much wood as you can load in your car, drive home, then stack it neatly (to avoid a lengthy argument with your spouse about that pile of junk in the center of the garage floor) in the corner of the garage. Rough-hewn or raggedly cut pieces of wood enhance Baker's Clay more than smooth and finely polished pieces, so salvage the rough and use the perfect in the fireplace or to serve as backing boards covered with fabric.

If you live near the mountains, the ocean or a wooded area, you'll be able to scrounge up pieces of driftwood or fallen branches, and you'll have the most naturally scarred and character-filled pieces available for use in mounting or displaying Baker's Clay. Take a close look at the simple shapes mounted on pecky pecan on page 31. The wood was so beautifully distressed and full of holes that it was left unstained, and even unsealed so the smooth and painted Baker's Clay pieces glued on top of it would show off well.

Five: (Fig. 210) Many projects, like this one, look fabulous mounted on stained or natural wood pieces. You can scrounge wood scraps anyplace you scrounge wood blocks. You may want to tidy them up a bit, removing dirt and cobwebs, but probably will want to leave distressed and scarred wood as it is. If you decide to add some color to the wood by antiquing it, you can

123

Figure 210

do so using dark brown acrylic paints and the same process used in antiquing the project on page 116. All wood projects need hangers. Before you glue the Baker's Clay piece onto the wood, turn the wood over and attach a pull-tab from a soda can to the back side. Push a thumbtack (or use a hammer if you have fragile fingers) through the tab portion or through the bottom portion of the pull-ring (see Fig. 211). Large or heavy wall hangings do require the use of store-purchased picture hanging apparatus.

Six: A good way to show off Baker's Clay projects is to mount them on fabric-covered board, like "Ol Sol" on the cover. The bright blue material I've used brings out the color of his eyes, and was a leftover scrap from a child's school dress. If you are a nonsewer, but have a sewing friend, trade her some Baker's Clay projects for free scraps of her leftover material. As a last resort, buy inexpensive materials which look good with the object you want to mount. Carry the project down to

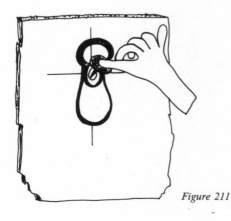

Figure 211

the store and place it on different pieces of fabric until you find one that looks just right.

Covering a Board with Fabric is Not As Difficult as You May Think

Step One: Gather up the material and the backing board which can be cardboard, wood, cellote (pressed-paper fiberboard from the lumberyard) or masonite (also from the lumberyard). Lay the backing board on top of your fabric, measure and cut the fabric 2 inches larger on all sides than the backing board (see Fig. 212).

Step Two: Sparingly smear thick white glue around the edges of the back side of the board. Place it front-side-down on the back side of the material (see Fig. 212).

Step Three: Pretend you are wrapping a package as you pull the sides over to the back and press in the glue. Do one side at a time, folding the material over at the corner, then do the opposite side (see Fig. 213).

Step Four: If the material is bulky, cut a wide "V" in the corner to remove excess material before you fold it over (see Fig. 213).

Step Five: Pull and fold the other two sides, stretching and pulling the material as tautly as possible (see Fig. 213).

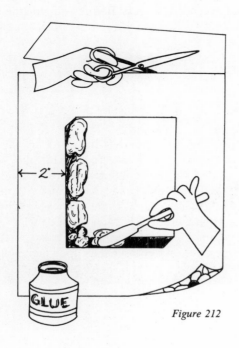

Figure 212

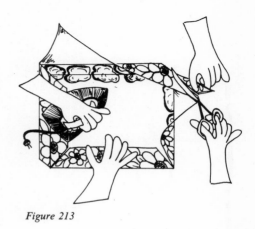

Figure 213

Step Six: A sure-fire way to hold the fabric down is to whip out your steam iron and press each side as you place the fabric over the glue (see Fig. 213). The heat and steam set the glue immediately, and if you use an old towel or something between the steam iron and fabric, chances are you won't get any glue on the bottom of the iron. If you're timid about using the iron, hold the fabric along all edges with thumbtacks, masking tape, or set a couple of books on top of the edges for 30 minutes or until the glue sets. Last of all, smear glue liberally on the piece(s), then lay it in place on the fabric-covered board. Use enough glue so it will go through the fabric to the backing board, holding everything securely together.

Store-Bought Frames

As I mentioned earlier, you can find inexpensive store-bought frames in many retail stores, some even painted or stained to look like you would like them to. "The Tortoise and Hare" (see Fig. 214) preparing to race are framed in an inexpensive wooden frame which came already painted a happy sky blue. Almost all picture frames come with backing cardboard (or glass), and all you have to do is remove this from the back side, glue fabric on it, (or in this case, felt cutouts resembling

Figure 214

Figure 215

Figure 216

clouds, sky and ground), then reinsert through the back of the frame. Then glue the painted and sealed pieces into place to finish the composition. If you don't like the color of the frame, feel free to paint or antique it to match the pieces which are going inside.

(FIGURE 215) Store-purchased shadow-boxes will insure forever-protection for Baker's Clay projects which have special meaning to you and your family. These pieces, fashioned by a houseful of crafty children, will be preserved intact now that they are hermetically sealed inside a shadow-box.

(FIGURE 216) Easy-to-find, glassed-in boxes are a good way to frame and show off a variety of Baker's Clay projects.

Home-Made Frames

You don't have to be a do-it-yourself builder to make simple wooden frames. All you need in the way of

127

materials are a yardstick or ruler, pencil, saw, hammer, small nails and lengths of wood measuring 1 or 2 inches wide by $\frac{1}{2}$ inch in width.

Step One: Prepare the backing board by staining or painting it, or covering it with fabric—just get it ready. Lay the backing board down on a flat surface and measure one side. Cut two pieces of framing board this length. Next cut two more framing pieces this length plus double the thickness of the framing wood (see Fig. 217). For example, the backing board is 10 × 12 inches, and the framing material is $\frac{1}{2}$-inch thick by 1-inch in width. The first two pieces should be cut 10 inches long. The next two should be cut 13 inches long.

Step Two: Paint or stain the frame pieces (see Fig. 217). Dry.

Step Three: Now assemble. First hammer small nails through the top and bottom pieces on a frame piece, aligning them exactly with the top and bottom of the prepared backing board. Then add the side pieces, hammering through them to the backing board (see Fig. 218). Finally hammer a nail or two at the corners where the boards meet.

Step Four: Affix a store-bought hanger to the back side.

Step Five: Glue the Baker's Clay pieces into place. Dry flat for 24 hours.

Figure 217

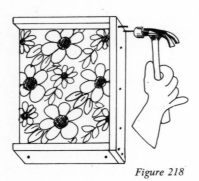

Figure 218

About Mitering

More complicated frames include those done by mitering the corners, which means cutting the wood pieces so each has a 45° angle to meet another piece at right angles (Fig. 219). I have never been able to conquer the technicalities of mitering frames so they fit exactly. If you have a woodworker living in your household, then you won't need instructions on how to make frames with mitered edges, and if you haven't, it would take at least a dozen pages trying to explain how to cut the wood exactly so I will skip right over it, leaving you with the thought: mitered frames are extra nice, but can be purchased. Amen!

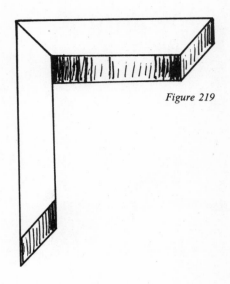

Figure 219

Combination Specials

Baker's Clay looks great mounted on almost any material, wood, fabric, glass, etc. etc. and looks particularly charming mounted on pieces with some stitching in the background. The felt background behind the turtle on page 45 is filled with simple plant shapes done with the running stitch and the French knot. If stitchery isn't your thing, try quilting a simple design to put behind the project, like the rain and waves behind and in front of "Hark the Ark" in Plate 23. "Happiness Street" in Plate 8 is a good example of combining all the framing techniques on one project. After the pieces were painted and sealed, they were glued to a leftover scrap of walnut paneling. This really didn't do much for the pieces, so a store-bought orange frame was added. While this color accent did tie in nicely with the orange on the buildings, it wasn't quite enough (shades of the Christmas Colossus), so a leftover scrap of orange velour fabric was put over a backing board. Then the whole thing was glued together.

And So On and So Forth

There really is no limit to the ways you can frame, mount or display Baker's Clay. Look back through the book, this time concentrating on how things are framed, and you'll find a wide assortment of techniques and ideas combining one or more of the ideas I've mentioned. You will be surprised at how many things you have sitting around the house just waiting to be combined somehow with a Baker's Clay project. For example, dig out those old Easter baskets, seashells, framed

129

Figure 220

Figure 221

pictures that you've almost discarded several times, or scraps of interesting driftwood you've picked up and saved for years.

(FIGURE 220) Last year Grandma gave our children fake birds nests (from the hobby shop) full of chocolate eggs. After the eggs were consumed, I salted the nests away in a closet. Several chickens got away from the project on page 23, so I glued one in an empty nest and stuck some weeds around it to give the bird an air of reality. This project also gives an answer to that age-old question about which came first, the chicken or the egg! Obviously the answer is the nest!

(FIGURE 221) The tiny round bunnies are sitting happily atop leftover blocks of wood. Small holes were drilled into the wood to hold straw flowers, then the rabbits were glued in place.

(FIGURE 222) Sturdy boxes, once full of Christmas cards, are just the right size to use in framing certain types of projects, like these pebbles. Cover some pieces of cardboard (cut to size) with fabric, and glue in the box, then position and glue down your project. It might be a good idea to paint over the words imprinted on the box sides.

Figure 222

About Storage and Shipping and Gentle Care

Anything made exclusively of flour and water is not going to be terribly sturdy, yet the pieces can be protected and should last for many years with a little care. Some Baker's Clay pieces, made hundreds of years before the birth of Christ, are on display in museums around the world. It seems logical to assume that if the Egyptians could preserve ornamental loaves and figures without the benefit of glue and varnish, we can certainly do the same using these modern materials and a little common sense. Seasonal pieces keep beautifully if they are stored in moisture proof plastic bags tied with wire twisties. Just in case moisture seeps in, place a handful of popped corn (without butter or salt) in the bag before closing: it will absorb any moisture and keep the Baker's Clay from becoming soggy or growing moldy. Keep this popcorn trick in mind if you make Baker's Clay pieces to send to friends or relatives living in other parts of the country. Wrap each piece carefully in pieces of corrugated cardboard (from throw-away boxes found behind the market), then place in plastic wrap with popcorn.

If you have field mice or other uninvited inhabitants living in the garage or attic, the first thing the critters will nibble on is unprotected Baker's Clay. All four-legged animals, plus bugs, detest the tast of polyurethane plastic, which makes dry-cleaner garment bags an excellent choice to use as a preserving wrapping for your finished work. (Besides, the bags are free.)

131

SO WHERE DO YOU GO FROM HERE 11

Or what to do when house and home and friends are overflowing with Baker's Clay projects, but you don't want to stop working in the media.

In the beginning Baker's Clay was something that gave me my "jollies" and therefore made me less hostile with my role as keeper of the asylum. Through a series of events much too complicated to cover in detail, enjoyment with the media and skills in working with it developed to a point where I had to find something to do with the quantities of work I was constantly producing. That something turned out to be making pieces to sell through a local department store that catered to customers who liked handcrafted goods. You'll never get rich making and selling Baker's Clay, but you should be able to make enough money to pay your husband back for all those little loans to buy frames and such, and should have something left over to "blow" on yourself. Selling will also provide you with a way of unloading extra Baker's Clay projects. Becoming involved in a commercial venture will force you to produce work at a constant rate, which will make you more efficient with your working time and better at your craft. Watch out though; it might turn out that you've got a tiger by the tail, and you'll end up burning the midnight oil to fill orders.

About Going Commercial

Some Things to Consider: In the first place, you have to be good at your craft. Don't take the first chicken you make and rush right out to a store to talk them into selling chickens for you. Chances are you'll get turned down and will have to drive home trying to recover your cool and get over the shock that not everybody loves chickens, particularly yours. Work with Baker's Clay for a while, try making lots of different things, and after you become really proficient with some particular types of projects, then venture out into the commercial world, Baker's Clay and heart in hand.

Next, selling handcrafted goods is risky to your ego and your very soul. It's impossible to separate you from the things you've made—and when you are rejected (as you certainly will be sometime), it's a very personal thing—and it hurts. I used to stomp around the house a lot, yell at the kids for an hour, pull weeds fast and furious or step on the cat's tail to vent my hurt feelings in the days when I first ventured out into the commercial world and was rejected. After the first couple of failures, I tried to take a less personal look at the rejections, figuring that a store's lack of interest in handling my work could be due to a number of reasons besides the fact that they didn't think the stuff would sell. It could be that:

a) They are overstocked in items of that price.
b) It isn't the season to buy angels.
c) Handcrafted goods don't sell well in their establishment.
d) They just bought 144 similar items from the neighbor that you taught how to work with Baker's Clay.

Getting Started

If you want to sell Baker's Clay pieces you've made, here are a few simple guidelines to help you along your commercial way:

1. Try to come up with some projects that will fit a certain need or could be sold in a particular type of specialty shop. This will enable you to really concentrate your efforts, although you may become bored repeating the same projects if you get into mass production. Spend some time nosing around department stores, drug stores, beauty shops and specialty shops in your area, getting some idea of what type of merchandise they carry and how you could adapt your work to suit their clientele.

2. Select retail outlets that get a good deal of foot traffic and that feature moderate- to high-priced merchandise, so that the buyers will be people who

133

have a little extra money to spend on frivolities.

3. Price your work realistically. Most stores mark goods up 50% . . . so in determining how much to charge for your work, consider how much it will ultimately be priced in the store. You will probably have to take less for your work if you sell it through a retail outlet. Some stores will buy the goods from you outright; others will take it only on consignment. This means you leave the goods, they mark them up, sell them, then pay you the agreed price. Try for outright sales, because the other arrangement can get hairy, particularly if some of your work is stolen or broken. Usually, your first time out, you'll be glad to make the sale, no matter what the terms; just try not ending up doing lots of work for nothing. After you've made some sales, and collected some money, you'll have more savvy on how to approach buyers for direct sales.

4. Buy yourself a little sales or invoice pad to keep track of what pieces you place in which stores, keeping one copy for yourself and leaving one copy for them. Ask your husband or a business-minded friend to help you set up some type of simple business ledger so you can make sure you are making money for all your efforts. Keep in mind how long it takes you to make what, in case you get an order for a gross (144) of something, and then discover that each one takes five hours to bake, paint and finish. With Baker's Clay you will have a hard time losing money, and your electric bill won't even skyrocket (especially if you cook with gas). What you have to figure is some sort of hourly rate for yourself, then use this to determine if you are being successful or not.

5. The Government always wants to get into the act, so be sure to check with your local Chamber of Commerce or City Hall to find out if you need a business license or resale license. The cost is minimal and a resale license will enable you to buy some of your paints and framing materials at wholesale prices.

6. Always call in advance to make an appointment with a store buyer. Explain what it is you have to sell, and chances are that you'll have no trouble getting in to see the right person. Most buyers look at everything and anything, and some will offer you advice on where to take your goods if they are not interested or don't think their particular

outlet is good for your creations.

7. Before you show your work, give it the old critical eye and show only your best pieces, or the "top of your line" as they say in the business world.

8. Once you make the sale, be sure to understand the terms of delivery and payment, get it in writing if you can, then go home and start baking. The final touch, which will help your Baker's Clay sell, might be a small printed card (handprinted if necessary) telling just a little about Baker's Clay, how to care for it (no washing) and your name, real or otherwise.

To give you some ideas about how to go about selling, here are some case histories of real people, who braved the cold commercial world, took their Baker's Clay lovelies to sell, and have done so, most successfully.

Case History Number One: (Fig. 224) Angela Shivers, age 33, married and mother of 3 school-aged children, is a Christmas- and angel-nut. She very happily makes Christmas things like this angel out of Baker's Clay all year long. She got to be very good at angels and

Figure 224

related paraphernalia, so she took her goodies to a very expensive department store, talked them into several of the designs and got a nice first-time order. The pieces sold beautifully and she now makes special handcrafted Christmas angels and figures for that store every year. In fact, they sell so many that filling the order keeps her happily baking up angels and baubles all year long.

Case History Number Two: Elaine Martin, age 24, married, a retired psychologist awaiting the birth of her first offspring, was bored being home with nothing to challenge her mind; enjoyed working with Baker's Clay, particularly making small circus figures like the ones in Plate 14. She took some samples of her work to an arty shop specializing in unusual decorator pieces. They now order from her regularly, keeping her happily creating charming figures, though she has now created two charming children-type figures of her own and doesn't have too much free time to create Baker's Clay.

Case History Number Three: (Fig. 225) Dorothy Henshaw, age 55, married and a grandmother, spends much of her time as a hospital pink lady (volunteer). The hospital gift shop carries handmade items for sale, so she created some lumpy figures holding a variety of hand-painted signs with messages of cheer and began to sell them through the gift shop. She took some samples to other hospitals, all of whom have gift shops, and now supplies her lovable lumpies to a dozen hospitals in a large metropolitan area.

Figure 225

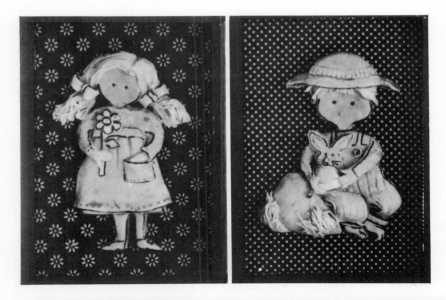

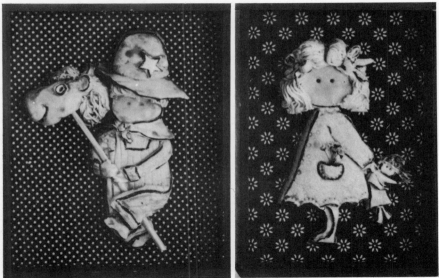

Figure 226

Case History Number Four: (Fig. 226) Charlene McMahan, age 40, married and the mother of two teenagers, against the advice of her husband and kids, decided to go into business for herself. Since she really didn't have any skills other than working with Baker's Clay, she hit the local children's clothing shops in her area, picked up some cute greeting cards, then came up with some Baker's Clay figures mounted on dotted swiss fabric, just perfect for bedrooms of small children. She now sells these plaques through several outlets.

Case History Number Five: Ebet Dudley, age 18 and interested in extra money for college and books, contacted a plush art center, took some samples to show, and would be producing puppets like the one on the cover full time if school didn't interfere.

Case History Number Six: "Bettina," an inventive lady

Figure 227

Figure 228

with several grown and married children, decided to really commercialize on her ability to make these miniature Baker's Clay figures (see Fig. 227). She travels the county fair and exposition trail in California, selling her Baker's Clay figures and taking orders for pieces to be sent around the world (see Fig. 228).

Other Commercial Ideas

When going through the selling phase of my creative development, the entire family participated in outside art and craft festivals (see Fig. 229). I would choose functions which were well attended and usually in fun locations, and we'd all go for the day. Glenn would help me set up the display board (a large piece of cellotex covered with bright green felt) and the card table, and the kids would help unpack things. Angels and Baby Baubles would be hung in a live potted fir tree and plant perk-ups stuck in assorted house plants. We'd all take turns sitting with the display while the others wandered around to look or shop. We'd have a picnic lunch, take turns napping under a nearby tree, usually sell out, then go home, pockets jingling and faces aglow with third-degree sunburns (did I forget to mention that one necessary ingredient for outdoor sales is a large floppy hat for everybody?

Figure 229

Figure 230

All cities, regardless of size, have charity bazaars or boutique sales, and almost all welcome craftspeople willing to donate some of their profit to the organization. Go to some of these sales, determine which one looks like the most fun or has the most people buying items, then make arrangements to be a part of the sale for the next year. Or, check with your local art and craft associations to find out how you can participate in their

140

open air sales in parking lots or in shopping malls, etc. (see Fig. 230). Your first time out, make a variety of pieces, discover what sells best, then next time concentrate your efforts in that direction

Other areas where you can share your abilities might be in volunteering to work with children's classes at school, sunday school, day camp, cubs, brownies or scouts. You will enjoy showing youngsters how to work with Baker's Clay and will be amazed at how quickly they "turn on" to working with the dough. Veteran's hospitals, children's and convalescent hospitals or juvenile detention homes are always happy to have someone come in to work with patients, showing them how to make useful or fun things with their hands. If you want to work with Baker's Clay and other people, you'll be able to find somebody to learn from you, so spread yourself and your Baker's Clay knowledge around a little bit, you won't regret it.

This marks the end of our sharing actual Baker's Clay projects and ideas with you. And for you, hopefully this is the beginning of a lifetime spent enjoying this delightful medium. We've been involved with Baker's Clay for just a couple of years and know that we have most probably only scratched the surface of interesting uses and designs. So you'd better be on the alert for subsequent publications like *Baker's Clay Rides Again, Son of Baker's Clay, Grandson of Baker's Clay Meets the Biscuit Eater,* or *Great Grandson of Baker's Clay Versus Godzilla and the Electric Boll Weevil.*

May the spirit of creativity zap you til your fingers tingle with anticipation, and welcome to the most esteemed high order of floury thumb, elbow and floor.

CREDITS— WHO DID WHAT

This Is Baker's Clay represents many hours of baking and crafting, done primarily by myself and gang of merry madmen, Jerrie, Jan, Marlo and Sandie. Without their creative ideas, Baker's Clay projects, and generally helpful criticism of the book, the whole thing never would have made it off the kitchen floor. We were fortunate to come across other happy little bakers who were passionately involved with Baker's Clay and willing to share their work with others. Their contributions to the book should not go unheralded, so here they are, along with notations on everyone who contributed.

Betinna Corson—Raggedy Ann, p. 138.

Ebet Dudley—rabbit, p. 26; "Two Birds in a Bush," p. 28; wreath, p. 41; flowers, p. 42; breadbasket, p. 44; Baker's bill, p. 72; houses, p. 73; rocking horse, p. 79; "Adam's Apples," p. 103; framed children's pieces, p. 127; painted wreath, Plate 3; "Madonna and Child," Plate 22; "The Band. Marches On," p. 104.

Carol Gibson—"Little Ol' Dough Maker," p. 7; "Dough Dolls," Plate 17.

Dorothy Henshaw—"Lumpies," p. 136.

Marlo Johansen—turtle, p. 45; "Car-Pool Queen" and Other Clever Cookies, p. 46; decorated box, p. 63; candle holders, p. 64; "Knights and Castles," Plate 6; "Gingerclay House," p. 66; ladybug on bark, p. 83; lady on log, p. 97; owl on log, p. 97; "The Tortoise and Hare," p. 126.

Val Lyles—sun collection, p. 45; angel with pie-plate wings, p. 90.

Elaine Martin—clowns, Plate 14.

Charlene McMahan—children's plaques, p. 137.
Betsy Mitchell—angel, p. 91.
Janie Nielsen—"Irwin Owl," p. 59.
Jerrie Peters—sunburst pictures, p. 31; hand, p. 54; snake word plaques, p. 88; "Happy Easter" centerpiece, p. 101; bunnies on blocks, p. 130; "Happiness Street," Plate 8.
Sandie Piper—lamb, p. 46; macrame wall hanging, p. 84, macrame holder, p. 85; carousel horse, p. 102; shadow box, p. 127; "Sir George" and "Clancy the Dragon," Plate 12; "Hark the Ark," Plate 23.
Marilyn Riding—gingerbread-like ornaments, Plate 1.
Jan Ruhl—Beauty on couch waiting for the Beast, p. 9; owl, p. 17; hanging rounds, p. 26; key caddy, p. 27; "Ol' Sol," p. 44; chicken on nest, p. 45; "Women's Lib and Friend," p. 53; covered jar, p. 58; snails, p. 86; candleholders, p. 88; mushroom ring, p. 96; sun face, p. 109; cow, p. 112; "Birds and Lollipops," p. 113; double basket, p. 121; flower on wood scrap, p. 124; mushroom cluster, Plate 2; hanging basket, Plate 4; "Victorian Villa," Plate 9; "How Now Bread Cow," Plate 15.
Angela Shivers—angel, p. 135.
Gerri Tally—gingerbread-like ornaments, Plate 1.

Acknowledgements Also to

My husband, Glenn, who gifted me with an electric typewriter and the Dale Carnegie Course—to prepare me for coping with the business world. His patience with unironed shirts and unmade beds has helped me to pursue writing and crafting with a reasonably clear conscience. (Actually, he probably plans to go on tour as a golf pro should I become successful enough to support all of us in the manner to which he thinks we have become accustomed!)

Our children, Penny and Charlie, who have good-naturedly survived my transition from Mrs. Clean, perpetually scrubbing, dusting, waxing, organizing and crabbing, to Mother-crafts junkie, unruffled by flour on the kitchen floor, dust on the coffee table, the growing ironing mountain, and a houseful of their noisy young friends.

Jim Piper, English teacher, author and friend. While I shall probably never learn the difference between a connecting pronoun or a perfect past participle, Jim's honest and helpful critiques have forced me to really work at writing.

143

INDEX

147